# Summary But Memoir | Readtrepreneur Publishing: Includes Summary of How Not to Die & Summary of I Am Not Your Negro

CW00351278

ABBEY BEATHAN

**Text Copyright © Abbey Beathan**

## Legal & Disclaimer

# Table of Contents

# Book at A Glance

This book is authored by Dr. Michael Greger who witnessed first-hand the ravages of poor lifestyle choices particularly as regards nutrition. His co-author Gene Stone helped convert his ideas in nutrition science into engaging narrative form. His discoveries and teachings in nutrition were inspired by Nathan Pritikin, an early pioneer of lifestyle medicine.

At an early age, he watched a loved one – his grandma – suffer various illnesses. Dr. Greger remembers how his grandma who was wheeled into Pritikin's clinic was able to walk out after subscribing to a strict regimen of plant-based diet and exercise. At 65, she was told that she only had weeks to live, but she defied expectations and managed to live to 96 years after making major lifestyle changes.

By the time he became a doctor, it was already established that indeed, *lifestyle matters*– that major changes in diet and lifestyle can reverse some heart diseases. He tried to advocate so. However, it wasn't an easy road.

As a doctor, he noticed that pharmaceutical companies incentivize doctors to dole out prescriptions. He was practicing medicine at a time when doctors earn more for prescribing pills and procedures. That didn't quite sit well with him.

Dr. Greger is not just any ordinary doctor (not that there is one). After having been accepted to 19 medical schools, he chose the one that has the most to offer in nutrition education.

As he was practicing medicine, he realized that whatever change he could make by giving advice on diet and lifestyle to his patients would only be a drop in the bucket. He knew he was saving entire families but that wasn't enough. He needed to do more.

So he started speaking in conventions. He went to so many that he eventually reached a thousand, practically living on the road the whole time.

Alas, it wasn't sustainable. So he sought a different way to get the word out. Eventually, he was able to get the word out through a website – Nutriotionfacts.org.

Backed by a foundation, he now has an entire team of researchers who help him comb through mountains of information. He and his team continued his research and this book was the product of their efforts.

The book is divided into two parts.

The first part is about the "why" – the reasons for you to eat healthfully. In each chapter, the doctor highlights how a person can increase his risk of developing specific diseases, and the role of diet in reducing said risks. Moreover, the "why" section also delves into specific food and how they work to prevent some conditions.

Chapter 1 is about how not to die from the top killer in the world – heart disease

Chapter 2 is about yet another common group of diseases that cause so much suffering – lung disease.

Chapter 3 is about brain diseases.

Chapter 4is about digestive cancers

Chapter 5 is about how to prevent infections

Chapter 6 is about how to prevent diabetes

Chapter 7 is about preventing the silent killer - high blood pressure

Chapter 8 is about how to prevent liver diseases

Chapter 9 is about blood cancers

Chapter 10 is about kidney disease prevention

Chapter 11 is about breast cancer

Chapter 12 is about managing severe depression

Chapter 13 is about prostate cancer

Chapter 14 is about Parkinson's disease

Chapter 15 is about how to prevent getting sick in the first place and dying from hospital-related complications.

The second part covers the "how" aspect. In this section of the book, he wrote about the kinds of food you can eat in order to prevent many chronic diseases. For example, in part 1, the author explains why greens are a healthy choice. And in part 2, the author explains the best ways to prepare greens, and the best kinds there is.

# Introduction

People generally die not because of old age but because of diseases. Sadly, most of these diseases are preventable. They can usually be avoided through lifestyle changes particularly diet.

It's surprising that although diet is a significant contributing factor in many diseases, it wasn't until recently that people and the government actually started paying attention. In fact, a recent survey showed that only 25% pf medical schools offer a dedicated course on nutrition.

The lack of importance placed on nutrition is made worse by the mindset of the modern man. Many people barely give any thought on how to stay healthy, in the belief that they could always just pop a pill when they get sick.

The average life spans of human beings have increased but there is a decrease in the amount of functional years that a person gets to live. A significant portion of our adult lives will be spent suffering from chronic diseases such as hear t disease and diabetes. The author put it beautifully when he said that "we're living longer, but we're living sicker."

In public school, students are now being taught about

prevention. Primary prevention refers to the measures utilized to prevent catastrophic failure of an organ among those who already have the condition. For example, those with heart diseases are generally prescribed with drugs that lower cholesterol levels.

Secondary prevention is about preventing the disease from getting worse.

Primordial prevention is a strategy developed to prevent entire societies from experiencing epidemics related to chronic disease risk factors. This involves measures that help you avoid acquiring the diseases in the first place.

In a study conducted by the Center for Disease Control spanning 6 years, it was found that there are 3 things that can significantly boost your lifespan – not smoking, healthy diet, and regular exercise,

Of course, aging also has a role in how our body functions. Aging is imprinted in our DNA. Strands of DNA make up the chromosomes on which there's a tiny cap at the end called telomeres. As we age, telomeres deteriorate until it completely disintegrates. Smoking and poor diet contributes to the rapid decline of the condition of the telomeres which indicates faster aging. Eating meat, dairy, and refined sugars are also associated with shortened telomeres while eating food rich in antioxidants are associated with longer telomeres.

A new study suggests that cellular aging can be reversed or significantly slowed through a healthy lifestyle. This can be done through an enzyme found in a type of pine tree that is known to reach hundreds of years old. It is called telomerase and it can be found in humans too. With healthy living, you too can benefit from the mechanisms of this enzyme.

This is what the book is all about - -- the choices you could make in order to protect yourself from conditions that damage your DNA. This book is about the things you can do to stay healthy at the cellular level and prevent certain diseases.

The author ends the introduction section with a promise that he will continue advocating using nutrition as a tool for healthy living and recovery, hoping that he will be able to ignite the spark that has led his colleagues into the medical profession in the first place.

# Part 1

# 1. How Not To Die From Heart Disease

In this chapter, Dr. Greger highlights how dangerous coronary heart disease is. It is the top killer these days, causing one death every 83 seconds.

Coronary heart disease is a condition in which the heart has difficulty pumping blood towards other organs because of narrow arteries. Over time, plaque builds up within blood vessels, subsequently hardening and causing the narrowing of the area through which blood can flow.

Heart disease is not merely a consequence of aging. Studies show that in some parts of the world, such as in Uganda and the Guizhou province of China, coronary heart disease is not as prevalent. In fact, in the Guizhou province where the population is half a million, not a single death among men below 65 years old has been attributed to this condition in a span of 3 years!

African and Chinese diets are very different but they do have similar features. For example, they both are centered on plant based food items such as vegetables and grains. These diets involve so much fiber and little animal fat, resulting to cholesterol levels that are very low.

There is so much conflicting information when it comes to coronary heart disease prevention. But the editor in chief of the American Journal of Cardiology, Dr. Roberts, argued that there is only one true risk factor for heart disease – cholesterol. Ideally, cholesterol levels should not exceed 70 mg/dL.

While the pharmaceutical industry has benefited greatly through the sale of cholesterol-lowering medication, the best way to prevent heart diseases remains to be healthy eating. Plant-based diets can lower cholesterol levels as effectively as first-line cholesterol-lowering drugs, minus the risks that come with synthetic medication.

## 2. How Not To Die From Lung Diseases

Suffering from lung disease is one of the worst ways to go. Just image not being able to breathe -- it's like drowning above water. There are many different forms of lung disease and some of the most common are lung cancer, asthma, and chronic obstructive pulmonary disease or COPD. Lung Cancer is particularly deadly, accounting for more deaths than three of the next most common types of cancers (*breast, colon, and pancreatic) combined.

Smoking has been widely recognized as a major risk factor. It exposes your body to so many free radicals that cause cell damage. Just quitting smoking will significantly reduce your chances of acquiring lung cancer and other lung diseases such as emphysema.

There are also food items that help keep the lungs healthy. One vegetable that has been proven to help keep lungs healthier is broccoli. A study on smokers showed that those who eat a single stalk of broccoli a day have shown fewer DNA mutations. This means that they are less likely to develop cancer. A study on inflammatory diseases such as asthma has shown that a diet heavy in vegetables and fruits greatly reduces the severity of symptoms.

Turmeric has also been found to be effective in preventing cancer. Turmeric is the Indian spice that is known for giving curry powder its distinct color, flavor, and aroma. It contains curcumin which has anti carcinogen properties.

# 3. How Not To Die From Brain Diseases

In this chapter, the author reminisced his childhood and how some of his loved ones passed away due to brain diseases.

Brain diseases such Alzheimer's are horrifying in that they, in a way, enable your body to attack itself. Stroke, a brain disease can suddenly and unexpectedly kill you, and Alzheimer's could send people in a miserable downward spiral that leaves human beings a mere shell of what they used to be.

A stroke occurs when the blood vessels in your brain get clogged, preventing blood from properly flow into certain parts, and depleting your brain of vital oxygen. Some strokes, called hemorrhagic strokes are due to burst blood vessels, causing bleeding in the brain and massive damage.

Sometimes, the interruption in the flow of blood is only momentary. However, these mini strokes, also called silent strokes can occur far too often and far too much that they would slowly reduce cognitive function until something more serious like full blown dementia develops.

Fiber has been lauded for its benefits for the digestive system, but it also has benefits for overall health. Fiber is associated with reduced risks of acquiring heart disease, colon cancer, breast cancer, and diabetes. Some studies suggest that it can keep strokes at bay

The author also suggests making sure that you take enough potassium because it can greatly reduce risk of stroke. The best sources are greens, beans, and sweet potatoes.

Citrus fruits are also associated with reduced risk. Preliminary studies show that it is likely because of a phytonutrient called hesperidin that improves blood flow.

The author also highlights the importance of getting quality sleep in preventing stroke.

The risk of Alzheimer's disease, on the other hand, could be lowered by the right diet. The Mediterranean diet in particular has been shown to reduce cognitive decline. It's a diet characterized by plenty pf vegetables, beans, nuts and other plant sources and little meat and dairy products.

There are also food times that have been identified to contain high amounts of aging toxins. These include BBQ chicken, bacon, and broiled hot dogs. Avoid these kinds of food as much as possible.

# 4. How Not To Die From Digestive Cancers

Three common digestive cancers account for around 100,000 deaths in the US annually. These care colon cancer, pancreatic cancer, and esophageal cancer.

Colon cancer is pretty common. The good news is that it's also treatable. If diagnosed and treated before it spreads beyond the colorectal area, the 5-year survival rate is around 90%.

Curcumin, the compound responsible for the yellow color of turmeric, can help prevent colon and pancreatic cancer. Those who already have cancer cells can also benefit from ingesting it. A study shows that turmeric extract can stall the progress of the disease.

So how do you know how healthy your digestive system is? Studies conducted in more than 20 populations across the world indicate that stool size matters. The bigger your stool and the more regular your bowel movement is, the healthier you are likely to be. This link is due to the time it takes for food to get through your digestive tract. Plant based foods takes less time to get from your mouth to your rectum, and that is a good thing.

Natural compounds called phytates can also help detoxify your body and keep the digestive system healthy. Phytates are found in seeds, whole grains, nuts, and beans.

Another digestive disease, acid reflux, can lead to esophageal cancer. Fat intake increases the likelihood of acid reflux while fiber intake reduces the likelihood of it occurring. There are also food sources that help prevent this type of cancer; these include dark-green leafy vegetables and fruits with vivid colors such as berries and citrus.

## 5. How Not To Die From Infections

Every day, we are subjected to a barrage of bacteria. They are in the food we eat and the air we inhale. Many of these microorganisms are harmless, but some can cause serious infectious diseases. Sometimes, you don't even have to be introduced to a pathogen in order to get sick. Sometimes, there are bacteria inside you, waiting for your immune system to weaken before striking. That's why it's crucial to keep your immune system strong.

Everyone needs to do their part to prevent the spread of diseases. These include covering your mouth and nose when you cough or sneeze, and frequently washing your hands especially after using the bathroom.

Keeping your immune system strong has multiple aspects. The first layer of protection is the skin. The second layer of protection is the antibodies that fight harmful microorganisms. However, as we age, our immune system starts to weaken. It is widely believed that weakened immune systems are just a consequence of aging. But that doesn't mean that we can't do anything about it. A study shows that people who eat plenty of fruits and vegetables have heightened antibody response compared to those who don't.

Some of the food items that greatly boost the immune system include mushrooms and dark greens such as kale and broccoli. Probiotics have also shown to boost the immune system, so much so that ingesting enough can prevent common cold. The Bioactive Botanical Research Laboratory has also declared berries as the ultimate food source when it comes to boosting the immune system. Exercise can also strengthen the immune system and prevent age-related decline.

Meat and poultry products are breeding ground for bacteria such as salmonella and yersinia, so if you're looking to boost the immune system, you need to be vigilant about proper sanitation and food preparation.

Many harmful microorganisms can be killed by antibiotics. However, the author also conveyed his concern regarding mankind's over reliance on antibiotics which may result to the rise of superbugs. To protect yourself from infection, do your part in preventing the spread of disease and eat healthy food particularly fruits and vegetables.

# 6. How Not To Die From Diabetes

Diabetes Mellitus is a disease characterized by chronically high blood sugar levels. This could be because your body is not producing enough insulin, the hormone that regulates sugar levels in the bloodstream, or your body is producing enough but is resistant to the effects of the hormone. The former is Type 1 diabetes and the latter is Type 2.

Type 2 diabetes is the more common form of diabetes, so much so that it is deemed the scourge of the 21st century, affecting more than 20 million Americans – and the number grows by the hour.

When ingested, carbohydrates are subsequently broken down into glucose. Your cells need glucose for energy, and it is the hormone insulin which allows the glucose to enter the cells. After every meal, insulin is released into your bloodstream, but if there is too much sugar or if there is not enough insulin, glucose builds up in the blood, causing damage in the blood vessels over time. This is why people suffering from diabetes also suffer from a host of other symptoms including poor eye sight, kidney failure, cardiovascular diseases, and stroke.

The causes of Type 1 diabetes are unknown and the treatment is insulin injections. Type 2 Diabetes, however is preventable and the damage could be mitigated and even be reversed with the right diet – plant based diet in particular.

# 7. How Not To Die From High Blood Pressure

The Global Burden of Disease study funded by the Bill and Melinda Gates Foundation showed that the number 1 risk factor for death in the world is high blood pressure. In the US, 1 in 34 Americans have hypertension and each year, it accounts for 9 million deaths around the world primarily because it contributes to a variety of causes of death including stroke, aneurism, kidney failure, and heart failure.

So how high is high when it comes to blood pressure? Normal blood pressure is around 120/80. Anything above 140/80 is considered hypertensive.

Sodium is the most notable dietary risk. Those with hypertension are advised to minimize salt ingestion and eat more vegetables. This is because too much salt in your diet causes boating/water retention, causing the need for your heart to work more, and raising your blood pressure.

If you want to avoid high blood pressure, you need to reduce salt in your diet. Avoid putting salt on your table to discourage adding any onto your plate in the first place. Second, when cooking, try not to put too much salt. Just bear with the taste for the first few weeks and eventually, the receptors in your mouth will be more sensitive to salt and you will no longer feel as much craving for salty food.

Certain medications are prescribed to lower blood pressure. However, studies show that three servings of whole grains per day will have the same effect as some of these medications. In addition, whole grains can reduce risk of developing diabetes, colon cancer, and coronary heart disease. Note that this only applies to whole grains such as oats and brown rice. Refined grains will have the opposite effect – they can cause chronic diseases.

Flaxseed, hibiscus tree, and nitrate-rich food items such as beets, Swiss chard and arugula are also highly recommended for those with hypertension because they improve blood flow.

Those with hypertension are recommended to subscribe to the DASH regimen – Diet Approaches to Stop Hypertension. This kind of diet is characterized by fruit, vegetables, and low fat diary. The author urges the reader to take the plant-based part of the DASH diet seriously and eat more fruits and vegetables.

# 8. How Not To Die From Liver Diseases

In this chapter, the author recounts an experience in which he encountered a patient suffering from liver disease. He was crestfallen that such a preventable disease has caused so much misery.

The liver is a vital organ. It is the largest internal organ in the human body and is where nutrients are metabolized and toxins are neutralized.

Thousands of Americans die from liver disease each year and the number is growing. It can be caused by infections, drug overdoses, drinking, and diet.

Preliminary studies show that unhealthy diet can damage the liver in as early as 1 week. Fatty liver disease starts with fat buildup due to poor diet. This can cause inflammation and over time, scarring which is akin to cirrhosis. This can lead to liver cancer, liver failure, and death.

Excessive alcohol consumption can also lead to fatty liver disease.

Viral hepatitis conditions are also common liver diseases, with hepatitis C being the most dreaded. Hepatitis C infection can lead to liver failure. It is usually transmitted through sharing needles.

Certain plant foods have been proven to protect the liver. These include whole grains like oatmeal and plants that contain the compound anthocyanin – the pigments that give certain fruits it red, purple, or blue color (grapes and plums)

Coffee also showed potential as liver-friendly food because it has the ability to reduce liver inflammation significantly.

# 9. How Not To Die From Blood Cancers

Childhood leukemia, a type of blood cancer affects more children than any other type of cancer, and is 10x more likely to be diagnosed in adults.

With blood cancer, the cancer cells are in liquid form instead of the usual solid mass of tumors. This type of cancer is categorized into three types: leukemia, lymphoma, and myeloma.

Leukemia is a cancer in which the bone marrow produces more white blood cells than usual, instead of red blood cells, leading to anemia, infections, and eventually, death.

Lymphoma is a cancer of certain types of white blood cells. The cancer cells accumulate in the lymphatic system.

Myeloma is a cancer of the plasma cells and is one of the deadliest forms of cancer.

A study done by researchers from the University of Oxford involving sixty thousand patients showed that those who are on a plant-based diet are less likely to develop all forms of cancers. Such a diet seemed to be particularly effective against blood cancers.

Cancer prevention and treatment is primarily about preventing cancer cells from multiplying while promoting the growth of healthy cells. There are compounds present in plants that can do the job. One particular compound is sulforaphane, which is present in cruciferous vegetables like kale, cauliflower, and broccoli. When observed in a petri dish, researchers noted that it can kill leukemia cancer cells. More importantly, plant-based compounds are not as damaging as chemotherapy. Chemotherapy is a crucial treatment procedure because it kills cancer cells; however, it does tend to damage healthy cells as well.

Extract from acai berries have also shown potential in combatting leukemia. The compound curcumin found in turmeric can also potentially stop myeloma.

# 10. How Not To Die From Kidney Disease

The kidneys get little love, what with heart diseases and hypertension getting more attention. However, kidneys are just as vital a part of the human body. They work 24/7 in order to keep your system clean and functional. If they fail, you will have to get a new one, or undergo dialysis.

At the time of writing, the average life expectancy of someone who has to go on dialysis is 3 years.

Kidneys are packed with blood vessels. Remember how the average modern American diet is toxic to the heart and the brain? Just imagine the damage such a diet is causing the kidneys as well.

Researchers from Harvard University uncovered the three things associated with poor kidney function – animal protein, fat, and cholesterol. Notice how all three are present in animal products.

It is important to keep in mind that not all proteins are created equal. The research also found that plant-based protein is not associated with such a decline in function. In fact, consuming plant based proteins that are of the same amount as animal-based protein causes less stress on the kidneys.

Animal protein is also deemed detrimental to kidney function because it is acid forming. Moreover, plant-based diets have been found to prevent the occurrence of kidney stones.

It's also important to avoid taking in too much phosphorus if you want to protect your kidneys. It's easy to do this – just check the labels of food items and avoid buying anything which has phosphate on the list of ingredients.

# 11. How Not To Die From Breast Cancer

Every year, more than 200,000 women are diagnosed with breast cancer and about a quarter will die from it. You will always hear about the importance of its early detection, but the truth is, by the time a mammogram spots a tumor, there will have been a billion cancer cells already.

The good news is, you can help prevent the growth of cancer cells by the right diet. The bottom-line is this: diet regimens that primarily comprise vegetables, whole grains, and fruits can reduce risks of developing many types of cancer, including breast cancer.

When you compound this diet with exercises that are as simple as walking every day, you can reduce your risk of cancer in just 2 weeks! The researchers attributed the enhanced cancer defenses to the reduction in IGF-1, a growth hormone that tends to boost cancer growth as well.

If you want to avoid breast cancer, it's important to avoid alcohol consumption. However, there is a compound in red wine that is believed to help suppress the activity of estrogen synthase an enzyme that fuels breast cancer cell growth.

The author suggests eating strawberries and pomegranates because they suppress the action of the said enzyme.

Nighttime sleep is also important in preventing breasts cancer because of a hormone called melatonin. Melatonin helps prevent cancer cell growth. This hormone's levels are usually at their peak from 2 am to 5 am.

Sufficient consumption of greens and fiber is also associated with reduced odds of developing breast cancer. Green tea is also recommended.

Soy has also been found top help prevent cancer from developing in the first place as well as prevent its recurrence in women how have been diagnosed and treated.

Cholesterol also has a role in the development as well as progression of breast cancer. Cancer seems to feed on it. LDL (bad cholesterol) in particular seems to stimulate the growth of cancer cells. Today, data as per the relationship between cholesterol and cancer is mixed but the largest study on the topic showed that women who have cholesterol levels of over 240 are 17% more likely to develop cancer.

A plant-based diet can help lower cholesterol levels. Broccoli and collard greens are especially protective against cancer, although broccoli's effects are more apparent on premenopausal women while collard greens reduce breast cancer risk in women across all ages.

# 12. How Not To Die From Suicidal Depression

Mental health is just as important as physical health. In fact, the World Health organization defines health as a state of physical, mental, AND social well-being.

That nearly forty thousand Americans die by suicide each year is a sobering thought. Major depression, a life-threatening ailment, is one of the most diagnosed conditions.

Contrary to popular belief, depression is not just about being sad. We all get sad sometimes – it's part of the human experience. Depression, however, is a prolonged period of sadness that could last weeks, and even months. It is characterized by diminished interest in things that would normally make you feel good, fatigue, recurrent thoughts of death, inability to focus, and weight gain or loss.

Research shows that meat-based diets have negative psychological effects; the opposite is the case with plant-based diets.

A review in the journal Nutritional Neuroscience concluded that plant-based diets can be therapeutic not just physically but also mentally. Some scientists attribute this effect to the

36

phytonutrients in plant food that inhibit the activity of an enzyme called monoamine oxidase (MAO). It regulates the action of neurotransmitters, and huge amounts of this enzyme are associated with depression.

Plant seeds such as squash, sunflower, and sesame seeds can also help improve mood.

Saffron, the world's most expensive spice, also has psychological benefits, although it wouldn't be easy to include this spice in your diet regimen simply because it is so expensive.

Physical activity is also associated with elevated mood.

# 13. How Not To Die From Prostate Cancer

The prostate is a gland the size of a walnut and is located between the base of the penis and the bladder. About 28,000 men die of prostate cancer each year and many men who die from prostate cancer don't even realize that they have the disease.

Some researchers from Harvard expressed their concern that milk may have a role in the growth of hormone sensitive cancers cells, including prostate cancer.

Some studies also show that eggs may be a risk factor as well. Egg contains choline, a compound that is associated with higher risk of developing prostate cancer. Ironically, the presence of Choline is used as part of the marketing strategy of egg producers and distributors in the United States. The truth is that the average American typically gets the necessary amount of Choline in their diet even without eggs.

The Pritikin Research Foundation conducted studies on how human blood reacts to cancer cells. The results showed that those who are on a plant-based diet have blood that can fight cancer 8 times better! The Pritikin Research Foundation also studied more than 90 men with prostate cancer, with one group being placed on a strict diet of vegetables, fruits, grains and other plant based food, and with the other not being given any lifestyle advice. The results showed that the men who are on the plant based diet had fewer markers of cancer cell growth in their bloodstream.

Studies also show that flaxseeds in particular are not only nutritious; they can also reduce tumor proliferation rates.

# 14. How Not To Die From Parkinson's Disease

Parkinson's is one of the worst ways to go, with many patients suffering a debilitating condition that renders them helpless for a prolonged period before death finally arrives. Symptoms include hand tremors, limb stiffness and impaired mobility. It has no cure.

The condition occurs when nerve cells in the part of the brain specializing on movement start to die. A history of head trauma is a risk factor, and so is smoking. However, more people are likely to develop this condition as result of the damage brought by environmental pollutants.

These pollutants include heavy metals, toxic solvents, fire retardants, chemicals form plastics, pesticides such as DDT, and substances that disrupt endocrine function. These substances usually find their way to our food supply, eventually causing damage to the brain.

Many pollutants can be found in meat and animal based products.

Hexachlorobenzene, for example, is a substance found in pesticides that were banned several decades ago. But traces of it can still be found in dairy, red meat, and fish. Those afflicted with the condition have also been found to have high levels of organochlorine in their bloodstream – a type of pesticide in the same group as DDT.

So how do you avoid Parkinson's? The answer lies in avoidance of animal based food items.

Coffee also seems to be beneficial. In a randomized controlled study, those who were administered doses of caffeine equivalent to 2 cups of coffee experienced improvement in mobility symptoms in just 3 weeks. More importantly, you should make sure to avoid head injury. Wear seat belts helmets whenever necessary, exercise regularly, maintain healthy weight and include tea and berries to your diet.

# 15. How Not To Die From Iatrigenic Causes

Iatros is the Ancient Greek word for doctor, and believe it or not, many people seek treatment in hospitals only to come out worse than in the condition they came in. This chapter is about how not to die from doctors.

Contrary to popular belief, modern medicine isn't as effective as we'd like to think. Many acute conditions such as broken bones can be treated. However, little can be done in order to completely cure chronic diseases like diabetes. In fact, conventional medicine particularly pharmaceuticals can do more harm than good.

Side effects from medication kill more than a hundred thousand Americans each year. 7000 die from taking the wrong medicine, and about 20,000 die due to hospital errors. There are also thousands of deaths caused by hospital-acquired infections. Laboratory procedures such as CT scans also expose the patient to radiation, potentially causing cancer. Even low-risk procedures such a colonoscopies are dreaded because of the pain and discomfort they bring.

This is not to say that you should avoid doctors at all costs.

Medical care is crucial but if you want to avoid being part of the statistics above, your goal should be to not get sick in the first place.

Two of the most common prescription medications these days are cholesterol-reducing medication and blood-pressure control medication. They are an easy solution to existing risk factors. However, a 2014 report on the results of a case series on patients with heart disease shows that a healthy plant-based diet could help prevent cardiac episodes in 99.4% of patients.

# Part 2

# Introduction

In part 1 of the book, the authors emphasized how prevalent chronic diseases are and that many of the conditions that pester human beings today are actually preventable by a healthy diet – the plant based kind.

In part 2 of the book, the authors share more information on the kinds of food that you should be eating if you want a healthier diet, along with the ways in which you can include them to your diet.

The matter of which food to eat is not simple. There are always benchmarks and other food times you can compare food times with. For example, eggs are animal products and are therefore less healthy than oatmeal. However, eggs are a healthier choice compared to deli meat.

The authors also ruminate about how some people think it's expensive to eat healthy when the truth is, many vegetables and fruits are so nutrient-packed that you are actually getting more from your money than you'd think.

The authors identified 3 major food categories according to source and processing, and then ranked them this way:

The green category covers the healthiest goods -- unprocessed plant food. You are encouraged to eat significant amounts of these food items.

The yellow category covers food that you should be careful with. These include unprocessed animal food and processed plant food.

The red category encompasses the food items that you should definitely avoid. These are the least healthy food sources: heavily processed plant foods and processed animal foods.

The author say that by unprocessed, he were referring to food items that did not undergo anything that may have resulted to harmful chemicals being added in, or nutrients being taken away.

Dr. Greger understands that every person's circumstances and tastes are different. It's perfectly possible for two people to have completely different yet legitimate diet decisions. That's why they were initially hesitant to proclaim their own dietary choices for fear of unduly affecting the reader's decisions. All they aim for is to present the science and let the readers choose for themselves.

**That is what Chapter 2 of this book is all about – a list of a dozen foods that are deemed the best of the best in terms of nutritional profile.**

# Dr. Greger's Daily Dozen

Healthy foods are not always interchangeable. There are nutrients that are found in some sources that cannot be found in others. That's why it's important to eat a variety of foods on a daily basis. For example, sulforaphane, a liver-boosting compound, can be found in cruciferous vegetables but can barely be found anywhere else. Flaxseeds contain lignin – an anticancer compound – in significant amounts but this compound is hard to find anywhere else.

Here's a checklist that Dr. Greger came up with after years of research on the subject of nutrition and disease prevention:

- Beans – 3 servings
- Berries – 1 serving
- Other fruits – 3 servings
- Cruciferous vegetables – 1 serving
- Greens – 2 servings
- Other vegetables – 2 servings
- Flaxseeds – 1 serving
- Nuts- 1 serving
- Spices – a serving
- Whole grains – 3 servings

- Beverages 5 servings
- Exercise 1 serving/unit

# Beans

These food items are associated with smaller waistlines and lower blood pressure. They can also help reduce cholesterol levels and regulate blood sugar levels,

Beans or legumes are loaded with protein, zinc, and iron. These substances are usually found in meat, but if you source them from beans, you will have the added benefit of other nutrients such as fiber, folate, and potassium.

Beans include black beans, cannellini beans, pinto beans, lentils, kidney beans, black-eyed peas, English peas, chick peas, yellow or green split peas, and tempeh

Serving Sizes are:

- ¼ cup for hummus or dip
- Half a cup for cooked beans or lentils and similar food items
- a cup of sprouted lentils or fresh peas

The author recommends 3 servings per day.

If you are from the US, you would think that it is it difficult to incorporate this type of food into your diet. But you'd be surprised to know that in other cultures, beans are a major part of diet. An English breakfast, for example, typically includes a hefty serving of beans. The Japanese have their miso soup and many Indian children usually have steamed lentil cake for breakfast.

Some of the most popular foods that are under this category are soy, peas and lentils. The average American is likely to consume a lot of soy, albeit in its processed forms – soy milk and tofu. However, despite being processed, these food times remain nutritious. If you want the healthiest soy product, try tempeh.

Peas are easy to prepare and are tasty to boot, which is why they make excellent snacks.

Miso is a fermented soy product that the Japanese enjoys. It is rich in probiotics, which is why Dr. Greger does not recommend actually cooking it. Instead, he recommends preparing the broth and other ingredients before adding the miso.

Lentils are also an excellent source of probiotics. They are nutrient dense but when they sprout, they become even more so.

**So how about canned beans? Will they be a good substitute? Studies show that canned beans generally retain their nutrients. The problem is that there is too much sodium in canned beans. If you have to go for canned beans, go for the no-salt-added variety.**

# Berries

Berries have great antioxidant properties that help protect against cancer. They also keep the liver healthy and your immune system strong. A study conducted by the American Cancer Society showed that those who regularly eat berries are less likely to die of cardiovascular diseases. It may seem too good to be true that such great-tasting fruits could be healthy as well, but they really are that good for you.

The average American likes his Apple and banana, and in the rest of the world, Mangos are popular. Those fruits taste great and have antioxidant properties, but the amount of antioxidants in berries is significantly higher.

The sugar content is also not a problem with berries. Fruits do contain fructose and while fructose typically causes a sugar spike, that is not the case with berries. Berries can even dampen the insulin spike that high-glycemic index food like white bread can cause.

One type of berry – the tart cherry – is known for its anti-inflammatory properties. Cherries in general can reduce inflammation in healthy people, but tart cherries are so anti-inflammatory that they can be eaten to manage gout. Keep in mind though that anti-inflammatory food items should be avoided in the last term of pregnancy.

Another type of berry – goji berries -- has high melatonin content. They can be used to aid sleep minus the side effects of most sleep medication. They also have high levels of antioxidants.

Black currants are known to help alleviate the symptoms of eye strain brought by extended use of computers

These berries also make great snacks. They can be served as soft-serve ice cream. Just whip up some frozen fruits in a b lender and you'll have some healthy 'ice cream' for a snack. If you don' want to bother with that, you can just add them to your salad or pop them into your mouth.

Dr Greger's favorite berries include açai berries, blackberries, blueberries, cranberries, sweet or tart cherries, and concord grapes, black or red raspberries, kumquats and mulberries.

Serving Sizes:

- ½ cup when fresh or frozen
- ¼ cup when dried

He recommends 1 serving per day.

# Other Fruits

The 2010 Global Burden of Disease study conducted by 500 researchers across different co0untries determined that the leading cause of death and disability among Americans is diet. And the worst aspect about the American diet is the lack of fruits.

Dr. Greger's favorites include apples, peaches, avocados, bananas, cantaloupe, watermelon, honeydew, kiwifruit, pineapple, lemons, limes, oranges, clementine, tangerine, papaya, passion fruit, black plums, pomegranates, and grapefruit. He also likes the nutritional value of dried apricots, dates and dried figs.

Serving Sizes:

- 1 for medium-sized fruit
- 1 cup for fruit slices
- ¼ cup for dried fruit

Dr. Greger recommends servings per day.

You have plenty of options. Not only are there different kinds of fruit – there are also many ways to eat them. You can have them as is, or bake them or poach them as in the case of peaches and apples. You can grill pineapples. You can also put them in a blender and enjoy your healthy smoothie.

You have to be careful if you have Diabetes though. Greater fruit juice consumption is associated with higher diabetes risk, although consumption of whole fruits is associated with lower risk of developing type 2 diabetes. This is because most of the polyphenols in fruits are bound to the fiber. Juicing is a process that separates the juice form the fiber, so avoid juicing as much as possible. Instead, use a blender or eat whole fruits.

Olives and olive oil are in the Yellow category, so intake should be minimized. Olives in particular have high sodium content because they are soaked in brine so exercise caution when consuming some.

Apples, mangoes, and watermelons are some of the most delicious and healthiest options you can enjoy. Watermelons are particularly good for erectile dysfunction. A study found that citrulline, a compound found in watermelon, can help combat ED if taken in significant amounts (about five servings' worth).

You can have some dried fruit as well. However, it can be hard to find sugarless and unsulfured varieties. You can also try drying apples yourself with a dehydrator or by baking slices.

Kiwi is good for promoting regular bowel movement and boosting the immune system. You can also add citrus zest to your meals to improve flavor and aroma.

Don't be afraid to walk into your local farmer's market and explore your options. You can do so many things with fruit. You can have them raw, blend them, toss them in a salad, chew dried fruit, and even add them to your cooking.

# Cruciferous Vegetables

Cruciferous vegetables are known for their sulforaphane content – a substance known to fight cancer cells. Dr. Greger's favorite cruciferous vegetables are radishes (Daikon and regular), horseradish, arugula, broccoli, brussels sprouts, bok choy, cabbage, cauliflower, mustard greens, turnip greens, watercress, kale, and collard greens. Wasabi also has sulforaphane content.

Serving Sizes are:

- ½ cup if chopped
- ¼ cup of brussels or broccoli sprouts

Dr. Greger recommends 1 serving per day. Horseradish has concentrated amounts of sulforaphane that one tablespoon is enough to get your daily dose of cruciferous vegetables.

Note that for sulforaphane to form, a precursor compound has to be mixed with an enzyme called myrosinase. However, this enzyme is neutralized when the vegetables are cooked. The good news is, there are ways to still get health benefits from cruciferous vegetables even when they're cooked.

Snapping or chopping cruciferous vegetables like broccoli initiates the mixing of the precursor compound with the enzyme. Also, while the enzyme is destroyed through cooking, the precursor compound and the final product are both heat resistant. So all you have to do to get the nutrients is to chop and wait for 40 minutes before cooking. At that point, the sulforaphane would have been produced.

However, this technique only works for fresh broccoli. Commercially available frozen cruciferous vegetables are typically blanched first is order to remover the enzymes in an attempt to prolong shelf-life. You won't be getting sulforaphane from frozen broccoli and other cruciferous vegetables. There will be no enzyme to start the formation of sulforaphane no matter how many times you chop it and how long you wait – the enzyme will remain inert. This is also one of the reasons why studies show that fresh kale can control in vitro cancer cell growth 10x as much as frozen kale.

You can also boost sulforaphane content in broccoli by adding mustard seeds while cooking.

Kale chips are also a great way to include cruciferous vegetables in your diet conveniently. Just use a dehydrator to make some. If you don't have one, you can use an oven. There are thousands of recipes for kale chips that you can find online.

**You can also use these vegetables as garnish.**

# Greens

Dark green leafy vegetables are some of the, if not the, healthiest foods on the planet. In the 18th century, George Washington rallied American troops to forage for wild greens. The American diet has come a long a way – and in a bad way – from that time. Today, only about 1 in 25 Americans even reach a dozen servings' worth of vegetables in a month.

Dr. Greger's recommends arugula, collard greens, beet greens, kale, assorted young salad greens, spinach, mustard greens, sorrel, turnip greens, and Swiss chard.

Serving Sizes are:

- 1 cup when raw
- ½ cup when cooked

Dr. Greger recommends 2 servings per day.

However, before you rush to eat greens, you need to know that you have to talk to your doctor if you're taking the drug Warfarin. This is because greens have high amount of potassium that can reduce the effectiveness of the drug.

Yet another reason that greens are so healthy is that they contain chlorophyll, a substance that works as an interceptor, preventing cancer cells from getting into our DNA.

Chlorophyll in plant leaves, even when they're ingested, has certain benefits for the human body. This is because certain wavelengths of the sun (red wavelengths) can penetrate and activate chlorophyll. It is this light activated chlorophyll that can trigger the production of a compound called coQ10 (coenzyme q10). CoQ10 or ubiquinol is a powerful antioxidant.

If you're hesitant to put greens in your diet because of the taste, don't be. If you find kale bitter for example, know that there are other varieties you can try. The author recommends trying black kale, red kale, and baby kale.

You can add a glaze (the author used balsamic glaze) if you want to improve the taste every once in a while). You can also add mint leaves for flavor. You can also add them to fruit smoothies. The sweet taste of fruits like mango can neutralize the bitter flavor of some greens.

You can mix them to prepare a salad. What will make it better is a dose of vinegar. Vinegar is beneficial in controlling blood sugar levels.

**There is, however, one green that the author recommends avoiding -Alfalfa sprouts. This is because many cases of salmonella poisoning have been associated with them.**

# Other Vegetables

There may be plenty of conflicting information today, but the one uncontroversial piece of information is that eating more fruits and vegetables is good for you.

We already talked about leafy greens, so this section will be about the other parts of plants or other plant food items that are usually not placed under the fruit category.

These include asparagus, artichokes, beets, bell peppers, corn, okra, onions, garlic, pumpkin, sea weed such arame, dulse, and nori), squash (particularly delicate, spaghetti squash, and summer squash), tomatoes and zucchini.

These also include different kinds of mushroom including mushrooms button mushrooms, oyster mushrooms, Portobello mushrooms, and shiitake. Purple potatoes, carrots, and sweet potatoes are also under this category.

Serving Sizes are:

- 1 cup for raw leafy vegetables
- ½ cup for nonleafy vegetables (raw or cooked)
- ½ cup of vegetable juice
- ¼ cup for dried mushrooms

Dr. Greger recommends 2 servings per day.

The most important thing to keep in mind when eating vegetables is to diversify. Different vegetables have different nutritional profiles. While there are compounds such as vitamin C that can be found across different kinds of vegetables, there are nutrients that are rarer. For example, myconutrients are only found in mushroom --you won't be able to find them anywhere else. Drinking tomato juice might be enough to get many of the nutrients you need, but drinking carrot juice won't have the same effect. Different parts of the plant may also have different effects.

One of the most potent antioxidant food sources is mushrooms. Mushrooms contain ergothioneine, an amino acid that helps protect cells from free radical damage. Ergothioneine deficiency causes DNA damage and faster cellular death. The problem is that the body does not naturally produce this substance – you can only have some in your system through food. The best sources of this amino acid are oyster mushrooms.

A study published in the Food Chemistry journal about 34 common vegetables revealed that there are 6 vegetables that helped fight breast cancer cells, reducing cancer cell growth rate by half: orange bell pepper, English cucumber, jalapeno, potatoes, radicchio, and beetroot. The same study showed that 5 vegetables – cauliflower, green onion, leek, brussels sprouts, and garlic—are even more potent in fighting cancer.

The benefits of a plant based diet extend beyond health . Such a diet is also associated with delayed aging. A Japanese study's results indicated that women who ate more yellow and green vegetables are more likely to have fewer facial wrinkles.

Just like with other kinds of vegetables, there are many ways to enjoy this group. You can eat them raw, mix them with salads, blanch them, or enjoy them as snacks and dip them in hummus. You can do the latter with bell peppers, carrots, and snap peas.

However, remember the two worst ways to prepare food – cooking and pressure cooking. There are however, some exceptions to this. Carrots, celery, and green bean seem to regain their antioxidant power even after cooking.

If you're trying to get kids to eat vegetables, the first step is to have them readily available in the first place. Put them in a bowl in your table. Studies show that kids will actually eat vegetables even if conventionally tasty food like cakes and ice cream are available.

You could also try positive association by naming vegetables in a fun way. For example, instead of plain "carrots", call them "x-ray vision carrots". Studies show that this technique works. You can also "hide" the vegetables by pureeing them and then blending them into food items like pasta sauce.

# Flaxseeds

Flaxseeds are rich in antioxidants and can help combat hypertension, breast cancer, and prostate cancer. You can buy them in bulk in most local stores at just a few dollars per pound. However, they have to be milled first if you want to get their nutrients. If you're preparing them whole, make sure to chew them really well. Storing flax seeds won't be a problem; you can store them at room temperature for up to 4 months.

Dr. Greger prefers golden and brown variety and recommends 1 serving per day. Serving size is 1 tablespoon.

Ground flax has a light, nutty taste and can be added to oatmeal, salads, soups and just about anything. Even baking won't destroy its nutrients including lignans and heart-friendly omega 3-fatty acids. You can add it to your muffins or make flax crackers. Ground flax gives a rich and smooth consistency to food, which makes them great to add into smoothies as well..

Ground flax is under the category of nuts. This might make you think that nuts in general are healthy. However, while many nuts are nutrient-dense, they are also loaded with calories. This means that you have to be careful with ingesting them if you're trying to lose weight. Most energy bars that contain nuts also come with a lot of sugar, which exacerbates the problem.

# Nuts And Seeds

Eating a handful of nuts regularly can extend your lifespan by up to 2 years. According to the results of the Global Burden of Disease study, lack of nuts and seeds in one's diet ranks third as a dietary risk factor for death and disability. In fact, not having enough of these foods in your diet kills more than consumption of processed meat.

Dr. Greger recommends almonds, cashews, Brazil nuts, hazelnut, pistachios, macadamia nuts, pecans, and walnuts as well as chia seeds, hemp seeds, sesame seeds, sunflower seeds, and pumpkin seeds.

Serving Sizes are:

- ¼ cup for nuts or seeds
- 2 tablespoons for nut or seed butter

Dr. Greger recommends 1 serving per day

A mix of nuts is already a great snack on its own. However, if you're getting sick of having them in that form, you can always grind them and mix them into your sauces. You can use nuts and seeds to make cashew Alfredo or ginger-peanut sauce.

They can also be used to make hearty stew, such as in the case of African peanut stew. You can also enjoy them in butter form and pair them with healthy fruits and vegetables (e.g. peanut butter and apple, or peanut butter and celery).

The author shares that his personal favorite is dipping fresh strawberries in a decadent nut-cocoa sauce.

There are many kinds of healthy nuts, but the healthiest is the walnut. Studies show that bit can help reduce the likelihood of stroke. Pistachio nuts can help improve your condition if you're struggling with erectile dysfunction. Studies also show that eating more nuts and seeds reduces likelihood of premature death in general.

# Herbs And Spices

Here's a simple tip when choosing healthy foods – those with vibrant colors generally have high antioxidant content. For example, a tomato with a deeper red has more antioxidants than those with a lighter hue. This rule applies to spices as well.

Turmeric, a spice known for its yellow color and strong aroma, has potent antioxidant properties, thanks to a substance called curcumin, as discussed in some of the previous chapters. This is backed by numerous studies. However, because turmeric may have drug-like effects, it's important that it be thoroughly studied.

The average intake of turmeric in India is about a teaspoon per day, and that's why the author recommends that amount as the daily dosage.

There is another spice that can amplify the effects of curcumin – black pepper. So it's a good idea to add this to your meals when cooking with curcumin. Black pepper works particularly well with brown rice, roasted cauliflower, and lentil soup.

The author shared his preferred way of adding turmeric into his diet – he grates turmeric root and adds it to whatever he's cooking. Sometimes, he adds it to his smoothies. He also likes to add it to soy because of the added anti-osteoporosis benefit.

However, if you suffer from gallstones, expect to experience some pain. This is because turmeric also facilitates the action of the gallbladder to pump out its contents in an attempt to prevent bile from accumulating. This prevents gallstones from forming in the first place, but the pumping action might trigger some pain.

Too much turmeric may also increase the risk of kidney stones because it contains high amounts of soluble oxalate, a substance that binds to calcium and develops a common form of kidney stone.

Fenugreek is another spice that may have high antioxidant content. However, the common herb with the highest concentration of antioxidants is peppermint. Cloves and amla – an Indian spice, also contain high amounts of antioxidants. If you have gout, have some cilantro. 20 sprigs of cilantro per day for 2 months can cut uric acid levels in half.

Capsaicin, a substance in cayenne pepper, may help manage pain syndromes such as cluster headaches. Ginger also helps reduce migraine pain. Ginger is available in powdered form. You can just sprinkle powdered ginger on the food you're preparing.

There are some downsides to using certain spices though. Poppy seeds, for example, may contain opiates that can cause overdose. Some spices like nutmeg has stimulant effects when taken in very large amounts (two to three teaspoons).

# Whole Grains

The author recommends three servings of whole grain per day – the same amount recommended by cancer and heart disease experts. A 2015 analysis of nutrition conducted by Harvard University showed that people who eat more whole grains tend to outlive those who don't consume whole grains as much, barring other factors. This isn't surprising considering that whole grains are known to reduce risk of heart disease, obesity, type 2 Diabetes, and stroke.

Whole grains include barley, buckwheat, brown rice, millet, oats, quinoa, rye, teff, popcorn and wild rice. For pasta dishes, use whole-wheat pasta.

Serving Sizes are:

- Half a cup of hot cereal or cooked grains, cooked pasta, or corn kernels
- 3 cups of popped popcorn
- 1 cup for cold cereal
- 1 slice of bread
- 1 tortilla
- half a bagel or English muffin

Dr.Greger recommends 3 servings per day.

A common misconception is that grains are inflammatory.

This couldn't be further from the truth. In fact, a daily serving of whole grains appears to reduce inflammation indicators such as CRP levels.

There's also the matter of gluten. Gluten is a group of proteins found in some grains like wheat, barley, and rye. This substance has adverse effects on people with celiac disease, an autoimmune disorder. However, it is a very rare condition, affecting less than 1% of the population. Some people claim to suffer from gluten sensitivity, a condition reported in a 1980 study. However, the general consensus is that non gluten sensitivity is a condition that is more mental than physical. There is, however, a study, that showed that some people have wheat sensitivity – and not exactly gluten sensitivity.

If you suspect that you may have gluten sensitivity, do not immediately go on a gluten-free diet. But if you experience celiac disease symptoms like abdominal pain and bloating, and irregular bowel movement, talk to your doctor about getting a formal diagnosis.

2% of the population may have wheat issues, and for those with none, there is no evidence that suggests that having a gluten free diet is beneficial. In fact, subsisting on a gluten-free diet may even result to problems diagnosing celiac disease. If you're part of the 98%, Dr. Greger recommends the trifecta of fruits, vegetables, and whole grains.

There are many choices in whole grains on the market. But whenever you go shopping, remember the golden rule – color is good. Choose red quinoa over white. Choose brown rice over white.

You can also buy whole wheat pasta. But avoid buying grains with these words on the label: 100% wheat, stone ground, multigrain or bran. This is because it's a marketing ploy utilized to distract you from the fact that the products are not whole grain. To verify if it's good for you, check the nutrition facts sheet. If the amount of dietary fiber is less than 20% of the amount of carbs, it probably isn't whole grain.

# Beverages

The Beverage Guidance Panel was formed to help the public become informed regarding the nutritional benefits as well as risks of certain beverages. The panel identified beverage categories and ranked them in a 6-tier scale.

Surprisingly, they ranked whole milk with beer, citing its effects on the hormone IGF-1 which may help stimulate cancer cell growth. Tea and coffee are ranked as the second healthiest drinks, second only to water, which has the top rank.

The importance of water cannot be stressed enough. There is little evidence that backs the notion that we should be drinking 8 glasses per day. However, one thing is sure: not drinking enough water can result to a barrage of health problems from fractures and heat stroke to heart disease, kidney disease, and colon cancer.

The author proclaimed that as of writing, the best evidence for a recommendation as to how much water is needed by the average person in a day are from the results of the Adventist Health Study in which 2000 subjects were studied. The results showed that those who drank at least 5 glasses of water are less likely to suffer from heart disease. Note that about half of these subjects are vegetarians so the fluid from vegetables and fruits weren't taken into account.

In addition, water dehydration is associated with poor mental function. It may also affect your mood. Lack of hydration may also lead to feelings of fatigue.

If you feel that water is too boring, feel free to add fruits and vegetables to a pitcher of water, or add strawberries in your ice cubes. Cucumber and cinnamon make refreshing beverages.

If you're looking for healthy sweeteners, avoid artificial varieties like saccharine and aspartame. Go for blackstrap molasses and date sugar.

So how exactly do you know just how much to drink? Dr. Greger's advice is to listen to your body. If you pee a lot so soon after drinking water; it could be an indication that you still have plenty of water in your system.

# Exercise

Dr. Greger. classifies physical exercise into 2 categories: moderate-intensity and vigorous

Moderate intensity exercises include: dancing, bicycling, canoeing dodgeball, fencing, downhill skiing, hiking, housework, ice-skating, in-line skating, jumping on a trampoline, juggling, paddle boating, Frisbee, roller-skating, shooting baskets, skateboarding, shoveling light snow or yard work, snorkeling, swimming recreationally, tennis (doubles), walking briskly (about 4 mph), water aerobics, treading water, and waterskiing

Vigorous exercises include

bicycling uphill, backpacking, circuit weight training, basketball, cross-country skiing, football, hockey, jogging, jumping jacks, lacrosse, jumping rope, racquetball, push-ups and pull-ups, rock climbing, rugby, scuba diving, running, tennis (singles), soccer, squash, step aerobics, speed skating, swimming laps, and walking briskly uphill.

Dr. Greger recommends either 90 minutes of moderates intensity exercises or 40 minutes of vigorous exercises per day.

Physical inactivity is deemed one of the (if not the) biggest problem of the 21st century. It is true that diet is by far the biggest killer, followed by smoking, but lack of physical activity up there in the list of risk factors of disability.Lack of physical activity leads to weight gain.

Exercise can help maintain cognitive function, keep your immune system strong, prevent and manage high blood pressure, and improve the quality of your sleep.

If your job requires that you sit all day, as is the case of most office jobs, consider your options such as getting a treadmill desk. You can also take a break now and then to engage in physical activity like walking up and down a flight of stairs.

Exercise typically comes with sore muscles though – after all, it's part of the process of muscle building. However, there is a way to optimize recovery and minimize downtime – eating the right diet. Eating blueberries can help with this because it helps reduce inflammation. Eating a couple of cups of watermelon before intense activity can also help reduce soreness.

Also, keep in mind that exercise causes oxidative stress. This means that in order to minimize this effect, you have to eat antioxidant-rich food

# Conclusion

Dr. Greger advocates preventive health. He believes that if you take care of your health now, you will reap the benefits later.

This is easier said than done because the food industry is constantly trying to find ways to get people to consume unhealthy food and engage in unhealthy habits. They are constantly trying to find new ways to tap into your body's inner reward system in order to give food that gives temporary pleasure, as in the case of sweets. It's easy to see why so many people end up with unhealthy lifestyles.

That is why this book has been developed. It is the result of years of research on the effects of poor dietary choices and how you can start eating healthy.

With part 1, he hopes to send the urgent message that so many diseases are preventable through diet changes.

In part 2, he shared a list of food recommendations that he is sure to be healthful. He also included preparation tips to enable you to get more enjoyment out of healthy food.

It is Dr. Greger's goal to help his reader realize how crucial nutrition is and understand certain facets of nutrition so that they can perform preventive care on their own. His nonprofit website NutritionFacts.org is a hub of free articles and guides that can help you do just that. He isn't trying to sell anything – no products or trendy diet regimen – just good advice on good food.

# Appendix: Supplements

Getting your nutrients form healthy food, especially those in the green category will also help you avoid exposure to harmful substances like sodium cholesterol and saturated fat.

However, in doing so, you might end up missing other nutrients especially vitamins A, C, E, as well as the group of B vitamins (thiamin, riboflavin, and folate). You might also end up missing important minerals like magnesium and iron.

To prevent nutritional deficiency, Dr. Greger recommends the following:

- 2,500 mcg of Vitamin B12 supplement to be taken at least once a week --You can also get your b12 supply from B12 fortified food like yeast. Check the labels when going shopping. This is the only supplement that the author implores the reader to take.

- 2,000 IU vitamin D3 supplement per day -- You may also supplement this by getting enough sunlight especially. However, during winter, the supplements in pill form may be necessary.

- Adding iodine-rich food to your diet-- Good sources

include arama and dulse. Some canned beans also have kelp. Check the labels for iodine content.

- 250 mg of long-chain omega-3s per day (pollutant-free)

The rest of the vitamins, minerals, and other nutrients you need can be taken care of through your plant-based diet.

# Final Thoughts

Hey! Did you enjoy this book? We sincerely hope you thoroughly enjoyed this short read and have gotten immensely valuable insights that will help you in any areas of your life.

Would it be too greedy if we ask for a review from you?

It takes 1 minute to leave 1 review to possibly influence 1 more person's decision to read just 1 book which may change their 1 life. Your 1 minute matters and we value it and thank you so much for giving us your 1 minute. If it sucks, just say it sucks. Period.

# FREE BONUS

### P.S. Is it okay if we overdeliver?

Here at Abbey Beathan Publishing, we believe in overdelivering way beyond our reader's expectations. Is it okay if we overdeliver?

Here's the deal, we're going to give you an extremely valuable cheatsheet of "Accelerated Learning". We've partnered up with Ikigai Publishing to present to you the exclusive bonus of "Accelerated Learning Cheatsheet"

What's the catch? We need to trust you... You see, we want to overdeliver and in order for us to do that, we've to trust our reader to keep this bonus a secret to themselves. Why? Because we don't want people to be getting our exclusive accelerated learning cheatsheet without even buying our books itself. Unethical, right?

Ok. Are you ready?

Simply Visit this link: http://bit.ly/acceleratedcheatsheet

We hope you'll enjoy our free bonuses as much as we've enjoyed preparing it for you!

# Free Bonus #2: Free Book Preview of Summary: Love & Respect

## The Book at a Glance

This book is about how both the husband and the wife can appreciate, respect, and understand each other.

This book has three parts. The first part is about the crazy cycle – why husbands do not love their wife and why their wives won't respect their husband. The second part of this book is about the energizing cycle – how husbands can love their wife and how wives can respect their husband. The third part is about the rewarded cycle – the real reason why both men and women should love and respect their spouses.

Chapter 1 – This talks about how love alone is not enough to make a marriage work. The simple secret to a happy marriage is respect.

Chapter 2 – Men and women hear and see things differently. This chapter talks about the coded message that men and women send to each other.

Chapter 3 – In this chapter, you'll learn why women do not respect their husbands and why husbands do not love their wives.

Chapter 4 – This chapter talks about why husband stonewall their wives.

Chapter 5 – In chapter 5, you'll learn how to break the cycle.

Respecting your husband does not mean that you have to be a doormat.

Chapter 6 – This chapter encourages spouses to be mature enough to make the first move.

Chapter 7 – This chapter is about respect and how it can motivate a man to love his wife.

Chapter 8 – This chapter is about the acronym COUPLE (closeness, openness, understanding, peacemaking, loyalty, and esteem).

Chapter 9 – This chapter talks about how important closeness is to women.

Chapter 10 – This is about how a husband can open up to his wife.

Chapter 11 – This chapter talks about how a husband can show his wife that he understands him.

Chapter 12 – This chapter is about the power of "I'm sorry".

Chapter 13 – This chapter is about how important loyalty is to women.

Chapter 14 – This is about how man can respect and honor his wife.

Chapter 15 – This chapter talks about how wives can get into the energizing cycle by understanding the acronym CHAIRS (Conquest, Hierarchy, Authority, Insight, Relationship, and Sexuality).

Chapter 16 – This talks about how a man values his work and how a woman can respect him by appreciating what he brings to the table.

Chapter 17 – This chapter is about the man's need to provide and protect his family. A wife should not belittle her husband's work.

Chapter 18 – This chapter talks about the husband's need to lead his family.

Chapter 19 – A woman must appreciate his desire to give advice to his wife.

Chapter 20 – This chapter is about the man's need to have a "shoulder to shoulder."

Chapter 21 – This chapter is about how important physical intimacy is to a husband.

Chapter 22 – This summarizes how both the husband and wife can get into the energizing cycle.

Chapter 23 – This is about the real reason why spouses should love and respect one another.

Chapter 24 – This chapter talks about the real reward of unconditional love and respect.

This book will help you cherish, value, and appreciate your spouse. What you are about to read is powerful enough to save your marriage.

# Introduction: Love Alone Is Not Enough

Do you want to be closer to your spouse? Do you want to achieve harmony in the household? Do you want to feel understood? Do you want to have a blissful marriage that's free of needless pain? Then, read this book.

The Beatles sang, "All you need is love." Well, that's not true at all.

Half of marriages end in divorce because love is simply not enough to keep a marriage going. Love is important, especially for women. However, what we all miss is the husband's need for respect. This book is about how the wife can fulfill her need to be loved by giving her husband the one thing that he needs – respect.

This book contains vital information that will help you save your marriage and build a deep relationship with your spouse. This book is for those who are going through marital problems. It is also for people who want to stay happily married until death. It is also for jaded divorcees, lonely wives, spouses who have been cheated on, and engage couples. It is also for counselors and pastors who want to save marriages.

This book contains information that's powerful enough to bring spouses closer to each other. However, what you are about to read is not a "miracle pill". Sometimes, the glow a spouse feels after reading this book fades in just a few weeks. They go back to the "crazy" cycle. You must practice the tips contained in this book for at least six weeks. This will help you make "respect" a part of your system. The quest for a happy and satisfying marriage is an ongoing process. It's never over.

If you're struggling with marriage, you should know that respect might be the missing piece of the puzzle. Read on to discover the power of respect.

## Part One: The Crazy Cycle

 He reacts to her without love

She reacts to him without respect

The major problem of the wives is that they feel that their husband do not love them. You see, wives are made to expect, want, and make love. And many husbands fail to meet this vital need. After studying the scriptures and various books, Dr. Emerson Eggerichs found the other half of the equation.

Husbands do not complain much. Nevertheless, most of them have one concern – their wives do not respect them. This is the reason why fifty percent of marriages end in divorce. When a wife feels that her husband doesn't love her, she disrespects him. When a husband doesn't get respect from his wife, he acts without love. This cycle goes round and round. This is called the "crazy cycle". The first seven chapters of this book talks about the "crazy cycle" – what is it and how you can get out of it.

# SUMMARY:

# I Am Not Your Negro

A Major Motion Picture directed by Raoul Peck

**ABBEY BEATHAN**

## Legal & Disclaimer

The information contained in this book is not designed to replace or take the place of any form of medicine or professional medical advice. The information in this book has been provided for educational and entertainment purposes only.

The information contained in this book has been compiled from sources deemed reliable, and it is accurate to the best of the Author's knowledge; however, the Author cannot guarantee its accuracy and validity and cannot be held liable for any errors or omissions. Changes are periodically made to this book. You must consult your doctor or get professional medical advice before using any of the suggested remedies, techniques, or information in this book. Images used in this book are not the same as of that of the actual book. This is a totally separate and different entity from that of the original book titled: "I Am Not Your Negro."

Upon using the information contained in this book, you agree to hold harmless the Author from and against any damages, costs, and expenses, including any legal fees potentially resulting from the application of any of the information provided by this guide. This disclaimer applies to any damages or injury caused by the use and application, whether directly or indirectly, of any advice or information presented, whether for breach of contract, tort, negligence, personal injury, criminal intent, or under any other cause of action.

You agree to accept all risks of using the information presented inside this book. You need to consult a professional medical practitioner in order to ensure you are both able and healthy enough to participate in this program.

# Table of Contents

# The Book at a Glance

The collection of notes of James Baldwin inspired the story, *I Am Not Your Negro*. These notes were meant for a book which he never finished. The book would be entitled *Remember This House*. Baldwin want to write this book to serve as a tribute to three black men who protested and inspired multitudes of people: Medgar Evers, Malcolm X and Martin Luther King Jr. These brave men were all assassinated as a result of their courage. And Baldwin was determined to reveal the truth about their tangled lives and their unfortunate deaths through his experiences. However, the tasked was finished by Raoul Peck. He created a masterpiece but not as a written form but as a motion picture.

Like the film, this book was presented with some summary of news, debates, TV shows, letters, songs, pictures, and other things which would help the reader to clearly understand the points of the story. But these were explained in the written texts. The following chapters will uncover the experiences and the struggles of the "Negro" during the segregation in the middle part of 1900s.

**Paying My Dues.** While staying in Paris, James Baldwin felt guilt for not doing his responsibility. The black people have suffered so much just to pay their dues. And to be able to do the same, he has to come back home. He reminisced the days when he was in Harlem. He remembered his happy childhood and his first experience of awareness regarding their color.

**Heroes.** The author had his own version of a hero although he never admitted. But it was somewhat distorted by the entertainment industry during his childhood. They narrowed-down the characteristics of a hero. A hero, according to them, was white and vengeful. And the black people were always represented by a scared and suspicious character in the background.

**Witness.** Baldwin called himself a witness. And so he thought that it was part of his responsibility to narrate the stories of Medgar, Malcolm, and Martin. He remembered the joy and the pain he had endured with them. They might have opposing opinions but their lives were somewhat parallel. And their tales were vital in the search of a reason for their demise.

**Purity**. Neither the ancestors of the black nor the present-day Americans wanted the Negro to come to America. But only the white people have executed the right to justify their disagreement through slavery and segregation. They invented the Negro problem to assure the purity of their race. They made it appear that these second-class citizens were mere cargoes whom they have to isolate or eradicate. There was also no space for a mixed person in that country. However, at this part of the century, progresses have occurred in the entertainment industry. It has succumbed to interracial themes.

**Selling the Negro.** Although hope has been apparent for the Negro, the discrimination still continued. The very same industry, where hope has been found, was also responsible for the hiding of the truth. Everything was distorted and misrepresented, especially the idea of democracy, to tell the people that everything was alright. Baldwin presented the possible solutions to this problem. And the best thing to possess was passion.

**I Am Not A Nigger.** Baldwin gave his final opinion. Nigger was such an offensive word. The reason for the invention of the term has to be discovered if the white people still want to use it. They were not niggers because they were humans. And the process of healing depended heavily on the American people. They should accept these strangers whom they have stereotyped and enslaved. Moreover, he redefined the word history.

This book will let the reader catch a glimpse of Baldwin's

mind and advocacy which was "to end this racial nightmare" between the black and the white people.

## About the Authors

James Baldwin (1924-1927) was a famous novelist, essayist, playwright, poet, social critic and book writer. In 1953, he wrote his first novel which was *Go Tell It on the Mountains* in which he won a large audience. However, he made an important mark on Civil Rights when he published his essay collections, *Notes of a Native Son* and *The Fire Next Time*, ten years later. Although he was born in Harlem, he lived much of his life in France to escape racial oppression and homophobia in the United States. He died in 1987.

Raoul Peck, with his interest on history, politics, and arts, made films according to these such as: *The Man by the Shore* (Competition, Cannes 1993); *Lumumba* (Cannes 2000, HBO); *Sometimes in April* (2005, HBO); and *The Young Karl Marx* (2017). He was born in Haiti and stayed in Congo, France, Germany, and the United States. At present, he is the chairman of the French national film school, La Fémis.

# Also by James Baldwin

*Go Tell It on the Mountain*

*Notes of a Native Son*

*Giovanni's Room*

*Nobody Knows My Name*

*Another Country*

*The Fire Next Time*

*Nothing Personal*

*Blues for Mister Charlie*

*Going to Meet the Man*

*The Amen Corner*

*Tell Me How Long the Train's Been Gone*

*One Day, When I Was Lost*

*No Name in the Street*

*If Beale Street Could Talk*

*The Devil Finds Work*

*Little Man, Little Man*

*Just Above My Head*

*The Evidence of Things Not Seen*

*Jimmy's Blue and Other Poems*

*The Cross of Redemption*

# INTRODUCTION
# (ON A PERSONAL NOTE)

by RAOUL PECK

Raoul Peck was particularly fond of James Baldwin because he was one of the authors who tell the truth through his stories. In short, a reader sees himself/herself in his writings. He started reading his works when he was just fifteen. Peck was born in a country, Haiti, with rich history of people who successfully defeated a powerful army, and halted slavery in 1804. However, this important portion of history was forgotten because the rest of the world thought that it was impossible to defeat Western colonists especially by Africans. So the colonists closed down the first free country in the Americas and revised history.

Fast-forward to the time when Peck was already a little child in New York during the 1960s, he remembered a large Oriental rug on their home. It has images of John F. Kennedy and Martin Luther King, Jr. At a young age, however, he was not yet well-informed on their martyrdom, their difference, and their imbalance. Peck admitted the fact that due to his ignorance before, he became "an enforcer and an actor" of a falsehood about a "single and unique America." Unknown to him in 1960s, when he was just a child, Medgar Evers, Malcolm X, and Martin Luther King, Jr.

101

were assassinated due to the awareness that there was something wrong in the system. Medgar Evers died on June 12, 1963; Malcolm X followed on February 21, 1965; and lastly, Martin was murdered on April 4, 1968. All of them were black. But it was not their color which gave the killers a reason to eliminate the three men. It was because of their desire for liberty. It was James Baldwin who introduced the truth about them and decided to expose everything on his book project, *Remember This House*.

The filmmaker drew inspirations from the things he discovered later in life. For him, it was Baldwin who provided the backbone for his craft. The author linked the black martyrs' assassinations to Haiti's history revisionism. He carefully put stories of racial discrimination and protest into narratives. So Peck is determined to bring this story, *I Am Not Your Negro,* into film and extend his reflections to other people and tell the truth.

# THERE ARE NEW METAPHORS:
# MEETING GLORIA

(BALDWIN KAREFA-SMART)

To make the film genuine, Raoul Peck met James Baldwin's younger sister, Gloria Karefa-Smart, who was living in Washington D.C. Gloria was a kind and rational woman. She was also fond of watching Peck's films because the themes were also part of her life. It was her presence which made the project possible since she has offered two things: friendship and a 30-page collection of letter called *Notes Toward Remember This House*. The book, *Remember This House,* was never finished but the notes presented were keys to Baldwin's life to be able to complete the *I Am Not Your Negro* project. Therefore, Peck thanked Gloria for her endless support and forbearance.

It was also noteworthy to tell that Gloria also shared a James Baldwin quote to Peck through a letter in April 2009. The quote said that there will be new metaphors, new sounds, and new relations. As an example, work should be associated to happiness, not to exhaustion.

# NOTES ON THE WRITING PROCESS

Since the words came from a collection of notes which was not intended for publication, Raoul Peck admitted that he did not know where to start. As a future film, the story should not be a simple narrative; it should be dramatic. He has to gather all the words of James Baldwin to become a screenplay. He compared the process to a jar full of unlabelled mosaic pieces. Each piece of a diamond must be placed in the best position to be able to show its beauty and relevance.

Several difficulties was encountered by Peck. First, the notes were confusingly constructed. Second, these contained a lot of erasures and corrections. Third, the film should be strictly consistent to Baldwin's ideas. Throughout the writing process, the filmmaker was able to peek into the author's very own process of writing his thoughts.

Peck further admitted that he corrected some of Baldwin's writings for clarity. One example was that he added the last name "Miller" to Bill. Baldwin also wrote "Clinton Rosewood" instead of "Clinton Rosemond." However, he promised that, with only such exceptions, the film remained faithful to the author's ideas.

**Lastly, Peck thanked James Baldwin for being**

everything to him.

# EDITING I AM NOT YOUR NEGRO

## BY ALEXANDRA STRAUSS

Alexandra Strauss reiterated the difficulties of Raoul Peck when they were trying their best to make the film remain faithful to James Baldwin's work. Moreover, a film should be clearer and easier to understand as compared to a written form. It was more complicated·since a film was a collection of images, sounds, and narrative.

The collection of notes of Baldwin was already a bulky material. Alexandra initially thought that the film will be four hours long. The main challenge herein was to compress Baldwin's thoughts into a shorter film. Fortunately, they were able to produce a general outline for the movie through the notes.

The next problem was the search for the images to be used. And when the images were found, finding the right caption and the proper sequences were another problems they have encountered. They based their audio-visual presentation on Baldwin's work regarding cinema. They carefully picked the films which were watched by Baldwin and incorporated it with the narrative direction of the notes. Their archivist, Marie-Hélène Barbéris, also contributed vintage photographs, films, news clippings and other things which were mentioned in Baldwin's texts.

She also admitted that there were difficulties in telling the stories of Baldwin's three friends. Since the book was not finished, it was hard to connect the lives of Medgar Evers, Malcolm X, and Martin Luther King Jr. to Baldwin's personal experiences. The movie was neither a tale about civil rights nor about the author's biography. They just have to touch those topics without completely ignoring the lives of the three men. They also asked themselves who should narrate the texts and the events with a tone similar to Baldwin.

But finally, the film was able to complete its form. They were able to combine their audio-visual arts to a dramatic narrative. At the end, she shared a quote from Jean-Luc Godard which says that "If directing is a vision, editing is the heartbeat."

_____

_____

_____

_____

**

In June 1979, James Baldwin, 55, dedicated his life to a journey. He wrote a letter to Jay Acton, of Spartan Literary Agency, to express it. He wanted to narrate the tale of America by sharing the lives of his three murdered friends: Medgar Evers, Malcolm X, and Martin Luther King Jr. It was 1955 when Martin became famous. He was murdered in 1968. During that period, Medger was also murdered in 1963 as well as Malcolm in 1965. He kept a thirty-page collection of notes with the title *Remember This House*. In this journey, he was not sure of what he will discover, what he will do with the discovery, or what will the discovery can do to him. Unfortunately, these notes were not published.

—————————————————————————————

—————————————————————————————

—————————————————————————————

————————————————

**One time Dick Cavett asked James Baldwin an important question in his show in 1968. According to him, things were getting better for Negroes because they were already present at all walks of life such as politics, sports, and entertainment. But why they were**

**still not optimistic?**

**Baldwin answered that there was no hope as long as people were using this eccentric language. It was not a question about what happened to the black man or to the Negro but about what will happen to this country.**

_____

_____

_____

_____

Martin Luther King once said, "Not only do we have the right to be free, we have a duty to be free." It means that we have to fight for our freedom because it is our responsibility.

**

_____

_____

_____

_____

# Paying My Dues

The author, James Baldwin, was bothered. He saw a photograph of a fifteen-year-old girl, Dorothy Counts, as she goes to school in Charlotte, North Carolina. Different emotions were on the girl's face, pride, pressure, and agony, just like any other new girl in school. It was particularly more important for her because it was a historical milestone. The crowd should be cheering with joy but their laughter was actually with humiliation. They were mocking her because her skin was black. In those days, other white children were protesting against desegregation. And the White American Council has advised that when a Negro child enters a school, parents of white students should transfer their children to other school. Such courage was particularly harder in the South. One woman from the South commented that God would forgive murder and adultery, but not integration. It was one of the horrors of segregation. It was not an easy task for a young girl, and it made the author feel ashamed. He thought that someone who was like them should join the girl. But he was in Paris while it was all happening. He was far from the United States, away from the real battlefield, dealing with racial problems of both the Algerians and the black Americans. If a young girl could pay her dues, it was also time to pay his.

Paying the dues was a metaphor to doing one's responsibility. So the author decided to leave Paris at that time, not because he missed the American stuffs: the food, the buildings, the places, the ways of life. The grandeur of the Empire State Building, the Coney Island, the Statue of Liberty, and the Times Square, cannot do anything to bring him back home. He instead missed his brothers and sisters; he also wanted to see his mother and all of his relatives in Harlem. The memories of his hometown hunted him with its memories of Sunday mornings, delicious food, unique music, and peculiar styles. And he somewhat hinted that the town where he lived was populated by black people. He was now a stranger to his roots, but he hoped that his relatives still remember him. And he was happy to come back home.

At seven years-old, the author reminisced the moments with either his Mom or his aunt. He was at home. He was watching a movie in the television entitled *Dance, Fools, Dance*. The actress in the movie was a white woman, Joan Crawford. However, he later went to store and met a colored-woman who looked like Joan Crawford. She flashed him a smile which made him realized that she, too, was beautiful. And the idea of that was unusual for him.

# Heroes

The author remembered his ten-year-old self while being taken care of a young, white schoolteacher. She was Bill Miller. She used to give him books and talked about it. Ethiopia, Italy, the German Third Reich, and the world, were their main interests. It was also through her that he was able to watch plays and films. In later part of his life, he admitted that he wished that he could kill one or two white Americans. But he did not completely hate white people because of Bill Miller's kindness and generosity. He instead thought that it was not their skin which dictated their beliefs and actions. Bill Miller, moreover, was also treated like them, a nigger, especially by the cops.

In those early days of his life, it came to the author's realizations that there was no actor on the American cinema who looked like his father. But physically, there were. There were Stepin Fetchit, Willie Best, Mantan Moreland, and others, whom he actually disliked. His dislikes were brought about by the fact that the actors were not similar to any person he knew: psychologically, behaviorally, or spiritually. They were acting not to convey the truth about them. However, he did mentioned one scene in *They Won't Forget* which molded his very own identity. A black janitor, played by Clinton Rosemond, was frightened by the fact that a

112

corpse of a young white girl was found in the area under his duty. She was raped and murdered. The striking resemblance of the actor to his father and his terrified face was engraved forever on the author's mind. Their people were not heroes in shows. They were just some nervous characters who existed in the background and who were objects of suspicion.

Therefore, the American cinema and the dominant culture distorted the author's view of heroes. For him, Uncle Tom (from *Uncle Tom's Cabin*) was not a hero because he did not revenge using his own hands. The author thought that heroes were white and vengeful. He disliked and feared them because of that. But they were not the only ones to be afraid of because his own countrymen were his enemies. The cinema portrayed it that way. And the cinema was a reflection of the place where he had lived. It seemed like the screenplays were designed for mind-conditioning. They seemed to tell the viewers that heroes arouse from crimes. And therefore, a crime was either not done or justifiable.

Fast forward to the time when Baldwin was old enough for a debate in Cambridge University (1965). He argued the case of Gary Cooper who used to kill Indians. He advised to assume that a child was born in this time of white supremacy. Without seeing himself in a mirror, he will think that he was similar to the features and to the ethnicity of Gary Cooper.

113

The child will cheer for him and will find joy in the killing of Indians. The child will later find out, upon seeing a mirror, that he/she was a deviation from the majority, that he was an Indian. It was painful to realize that he does not belong to the society and will be classified as an enemy. The same thing could be applied to a Negro child.

After some events in his life, Baldwin wrote again to Jay Acton. He told him that he will write his book project and will begin writing in September. He will travel to the South to be able to meet some people. St. Paul called it "a cloud of witnesses." He wanted to see Myrlie Evers and her grown-up children. He will then return to Atlanta, to Selma, and to Birmingham. He will visit Coretta Scott King and Martin's children. Martin's daughter and Malcolm's oldest daughter were both in the theater. They might be friends and might be visited too. He will visit Malcolm's widow, Betty Shabazz, and their five children. Lastly, he told him that he volunteered himself as another witness to the three men's lives and deaths.

# Witness

Malcolm X was the first person met by James Baldwin. Baldwin was lecturing in New York while Malcolm was sitting in the first row in a quite awkward position. Malcolm was too tall. So when he bent forward, he can touched his ankles. He seemed to mistrust Malcolm because he only knew him through stories. The white people called him "the torch" because of some funny reasons. But Malcolm also has the right to doubt Baldwin. At that time, he never took his eyes away from the lecturer which somewhat scared Baldwin.

Medgar, on the other hand, asked Baldwin to join him on his investigation. As a member of the National Association for the Advancement of Colored People (NAACP), he was asked by black people to investigate the murder of a black man. The author was terrified of the task, but later realized that the endeavor has helped him defined the word "witness." He mentioned that there was a very thin border line between an actor and a witness. Only a single belief can separate you from a certain group. In the case of the three, Baldwin was not a Black Muslim, a Christian, nor a member of the NAACP, because of some reasons. Specifically and respectively, he believed that not all white Americans were wicked; he knew that their oppressors did not live according to the Christian commandment; and he stereotyped that the

115

NAACP was responsible or related to blacks' own version of a caste system. Although they have shared some similar ideas and protest, he was just a spectator at those times. There were things that he never did but they did. For example, he did not bear the pain of the criminal situation in Mississippi; he did not contribute to a group's budget; he did not organize nonviolent rallies and prayer meetings; and he did not shoulder the responsibility of deciding for other people's lives. He was not even in the country during those times. But now, he was a witness himself who has the duty to tell the truth, to write a story, and to share it.

And so Baldwin dared to tell the stories of the three.

It was obvious to say that Malcolm and Martin have opposing philosophies. They have crossed paths in a television show in 1963 in which Baldwin was also present. Dr. Kenneth Clark asked for their beliefs and their actions regarding the Negro struggle. They have opposing views and have undergone a debate. Malcolm X blamed the "ignorant Negro preachers" for their fate who told them to turn the other cheek to the offender instead of fighting back. He was one of the most famous members of the Black Muslim philosophy. And he was referring to people like Martin when he said "ignorant Negro preachers." Martin, on the other hand, have argued about the essence of love in this struggle.

Love was more than just a feeling; it gives strength and direction. Martin also highlighted the difference between nonresistance and nonviolent resistance to oppressors. Nonviolent protests were his suggestion to get rid of the Negro struggle. It did not mean that they never have done or will not do anything important to change the system. But Malcolm called him as "a modern or religious Uncle Tom" who would just keep his fellows unarmed and tamed. As a response, Martin argued that anyone who believed and knew the nonresistance philosophy can face any violent mean of oppression without doing the same thing on their enemies. He believed that when one received violence, it was not a necessity to do violence towards the oppressors.

Moreover, Malcolm X also said in that same show that there was a need for an organization which will not be approved by the white people. This organization will do actions of whatever means. And therefore, Baldwin once thought that he was a racist. Baldwin admitted that it could have been he who was "the Great Black Hope of the Great White Father" because he was not a racist. But he later concluded that both Malcolm and he were just victims of the situation. Baldwin actually admired Malcolm. He commented in the show that whenever Malcolm or other Black Muslim ministers talked, they seemed to be sympathizing to the Negro people for their suffering. Their suffering was a reality which cannot be denied. And that was Malcolm's power. In a society where it was difficult to express oneself, Malcolm was a refuge. He has the ability to let a person feel that he exists.

And although Malcolm and Martin have different beliefs, it seemed to occur that they have taken the same role. Martin inherited Malcolm's position when he died earlier in 1965. And for Baldwin, they have occupied the exact same role the moment they have died. They serve as inspirations for the multitude of Americans. Medgar would be very glad to witness it because he was the youngest of them all. But he was unable to observe.

He discovered the bad news while driving in Puerto Rico and listening to radio. The bad news was announced the moment the music stopped. Medgar was already dead. And so a flashback was a necessity to see him one last time. Baldwin reminisced his last moments with Medgar Evers. The latter asked him to autograph his books and drove him to the airport. He also remembered Myrlie Evers, his wife, as she waved at him. He also thought some of their conversations. Baldwin remembered how he pronounced road as "ro-aad;" and how he admitted his uneasiness every time he had to pass the tree in which a person was once hanged.

It also bothered him how his wife and his children have seen him shot in the garage of his home. And Baldwin was bothered because he was the oldest of them all; and he should had died first. But none of these men lived up to forty.

At that moment of Medgar's untimely death, he could not cry. It was expected to everyone who fought in this battle. Unfortunately, this country preferred a white hero than a black one. A black nationalist was not a nationalist but just a "raving maniac." He revealed that the truth was that this country did not know the future of the Negro race. And anything they did could be "the final solution."

Medgar's burial and legacy was compared to that of a king. And Bob Dylan dedicated a song for him: that at the end of the day, the epitaph will say that he was "only a pawn in their game."

It was also noteworthy to add another character in this tale of America. She was a woman named Lorraine Hansberry who was the author of *A Raisin in the Sun*. She was present in the popular Bobby Kennedy meeting in which Baldwin was both an actor and a witness. It happened just before Medgar was assassinated. At this time, she was thirty-three; she was only allowed to live until thirty-four. Baldwin also missed her. It was one of the few times Baldwin personally saw her. The group told Bobby Kennedy to ask his brother, the president, to join a little black girl as she goes to school that day or tomorrow. They argued that the act was a statement that "whoever spits on that child will be spitting on the nation." But for Bobby, it was a nonsense act. Lorraine, however, demanded from him a moral duty and narrated the incident involving a photograph in which a cop was caught standing on the Negro woman's neck in Birmingham. She ended it with a smile and said goodbye to the Attorney General as she exited the room.

Birmingham has been an important place in the history of the Negro struggle. To know the reason why, will require one to look at Lorraine's argument. The situation there shocked the white Americans; but the black people were used to it. The white people wanted to know if this was real. Or if it was happening throughout the whole nation. But if they were reassured, an action cannot be expected. This lack of concern was discussed by Baldwin in the Florida Forum in 1963. The major and negative effect of segregation was that neither the white nor the black people know what was occurring at the other sides. They were separated from all walks of life. There will be no basis of hatred when the white people were ignorant and unconcerned of the black people. Moreover, very few wanted to know what were happening on the other side. They remained ignorant of each other. So in contrast to the popular white American belief, the Negro people were never naive nor submissive. They were more than just a group of people who sing and dance in the embankment. They have been battling against a violent nation to survive. They were restless. They were never happy nor satisfied with their fate.

The Negro was an American. Baldwin proclaimed it in the documentary film, *Baldwin's Nigger* (1969). One was born in this nation and was used to its culture. There was no doubt on a person's identity. But when that Negro tried to tell the world that he had the right to exist, he opposes a system which has been accepted for such a long time and has been viewed as the absolute truth. He said this because the result of this struggle happened to him in 1966. He was declared as a dangerous individual and was included in the security index by the Federal Bureau of Investigation (FBI). It stated that he was a famous individual whose work concerns the relationships between black and white. He was defined as a Negro writer, who was born in New York City but lived in Europe, and a possible homosexual. According to J. Edgar Hoover, their only one goal was the extermination of crimes. But none of the information regarding Baldwin was a criminal offense.

The laws were not the problem because there were laws for

their rights. It was stated in the Civil Rights. The problem seemed to be the unacceptability of the white Americans of the fact that the Negro people were their brothers. And even if they did understand their relationships, they will not bother to do anything to alter the system. Baldwin made it clearer by comparing themselves to the outcast child of a family. The child was part of the "great Western house" but the other members did not like him.

Moreover, the color of skin was not the only basis of the white people's judgment. The blood that runs through one's vein, although covered by the skin, was also another thing. As an example, a scenario in the drama *The Imitation of Life* (1934) was inserted to show the status of the black and the mixed people during those times. One rainy day, a colored mother went to school to fetch her daughter. The teacher suspected that she might have been mistaken because she does not have any colored pupil. But then the mother pointed her little white girl. Murmurs were heard from her classmates because they have no idea that the girl was colored. And so little Peola, instead of thanking her mother, shouted and hated her mother. Purity was another problem faced by Americans during those years.

# Purity

The Negro forefathers never demanded to go in America. But the present white Americans too do not want their presence. And so they have created this brutal system as an excuse to their fate. Baldwin blamed the white people's unsuccessful private life that they turned into condemning this black people. And they called it "the Negro problem." One particular scene in *No Way Out* (1950) echoed this struggle of the Negro. A black doctor, played by Sidney Poitier, in the film attended two white criminals in a prison ward. The criminals were brothers. They kept on teasing the doctor because of being a Negro. When one of them died, the remaining brother blamed the black doctor for its death and called it a murder. He more than just associate the Negro to incompetence, but to criminality. But in fact, it was he and his brother who were criminals in the first place. But the whole community did not judge the criminal. They actually took side on him.

The Negro problem was not a discovery because it never existed; it was a mere invention because the white people wanted to protect the purity of their race. This invention has been converting them into brutes and has been destroying them. The problem was not made because of the actions of the black people, but because of the conduct of the whites and the stereotypes they have made.

And so Baldwin shared an anecdote with a blond girl he never befriended a long time ago. They were neighbors, but they never walked together. He never did because it was safer. It was quite ironic, but it was real. When he had to go out, he had to wait for five minutes after the girl had left their house before he could start walking. Both of them would walk alone and would take different routes. If they saw each other in the same place, they will not greet nor sit beside each other. Dealing with a black person was more dangerous than being alone because of immature judgments. The relationship which could blossomed between them, whether romantic or filial, was stopped even before it was allowed to start. As what have said earlier, it was for the conservation of their pure race. And white Americans should realize that it was wrong.

There was this show in 1958 which reflected the dilemma. Tony Curtis and Sidney Poitier fought against each other in the *Defiant Ones*. Whatever have occurred before the fight scene, the excerpt no longer showed. But it was stated that the assumption of the story was hard to accept. That the black hated the white due to mere anger and that he wanted to get him out of his life violently. And this misunderstanding was the basis of the white man's hatred. The white man already knew the things he should fear in his mind. And this fears were associated to the image of a black man. He thought that he was facing a horrific creature who was stranger to him. And so it resulted to endless negative speculations which were not real. The ideal scene for the show depended on the people who were watching. When Sidney, the black actor, jumped off the train, the white people rejoiced. The black, on the other hand, called him a fool. But for Baldwin, it was a statement that the black people did not hate the white people because of what they have done. They knew that the white people were also humans who could commit mistakes.

The black people have lost everything in this country. That includes their fellow black man being portrayed in the wrong sense in the cinema. For example in the popular culture, black men were portrayed as if they had no sexual machinery. And although Sidney Poitier and Harry Belafonte have became sex symbols in the Hollywood, they were used less in such kind of themes. *Guess Who's Coming to Dinner* was another show which was loathed by the black people. They hated the show because they thought Sidney was used inappropriately in the interracial kiss. In, *In The Heat of the Night* (1967), Sidney got a light kiss from another white actor. Men during that time do not kiss each other. But for Baldwin, it was a milepost. And in reality, it should start as soon as possible. It symbolized the future agreement and unity of the two colors.

Although the black people were still discriminated during those years, *The Secret of Selling a Negro* was aired in 1954. This film was meant to promote the selling of goods and services to the Negro people. It was called "the Negro market." It said that Negro families have progressed in this part of the century. They have enjoyed a lot of things which they were once deprived of. Since 1940, in San Francisco, the Negro market has escalated to 89 percent. The progress in the black people's lives was announced and validated by Bobby Kennedy. Although slower than the ideal, the important part was that there was progress. He predicted that in the near future, maybe forty years, a black president will be elected. This statement seemed to be a hope. But in the Cambridge University Debate in 1965, Baldwin cleared that this statement was welcomed with disappointment by the white people. They might have thought that Bobby Kennedy aspired of becoming the next president. For four hundred years, the black people were already in the country without any educational nor political opportunity. Now it was more impossible for a Negro to be president in just forty years.

# Selling the Negro

In addition, James Baldwin pointed out the essence of cheap labor, provided by the Negro people, in the construction of the nation's infrastructure. Therefore, the black people were more than just a race who should prove their own identity as they were already the ones who build this nation. Baldwin also had to accept that his ancestors were both black and white. To say otherwise will push the people to destroy the government. He argued that again in the Cambridge University Debate in 1965.

At that time, two hundred thousand American citizens marched to the capital for freedom and for jobs. So David Schoenburn interviewed seven entertainers or artists to represent the struggles of this people in 1963. He particularly asked Harry Belafonte if the event should result to a course of action. The latter replied that if anything should be done, it will depend heavily on the white population who have refused to help them. He did not say it exactly. But his point became clearer when instead of listening to the Negro's complaints and addressing their problems, the black community just received a series of apologies from famous American people. It included Richard Nixon, Larry Craig, Rahm Emmanuel, Arnold Schwarzenegger, John Rowland, Bill Clinton, Ronald Reagan, Todd Akin, Hillary Clinton,

Donald Trump, John Ensign, Anthony Weiner, Robert Bentley, and Thomas Jackson. Donald Trump specifically said, "I am sorry I did this to you, but you have to get used to it. It's one of those little problems in life." Trump's opinion summed up the Americans' reply to Belafonte.

Baldwin spoke that he was part of a complicated democratic country. To add in this complexity, this country have some American virtues. One was simplicity with sincerity. And so the apologies above, if believed to be sincere, have been accepted. Immaturity was also treated as a virtue. John Wayne, for example who warned and scared Indians on screen, does not need to man up. In *Trisha Goddard Show*, a mother admitted that she thought people will degrade her daughters if they will have a black partner in the future. These were some sort of immaturity. But these were acceptable.

But Malcolm's belief and actions were not acceptable. While Baldwin was in London, he received a phone call. His sister, Gloria, was the one who listened. When she came to inform her brother, she was acting strange. Malcolm was killed...

To remember him, Baldwin was tasked to work on the screenplay of *The Autobiography of Malcolm X*. It was difficult for he personally knew the subject. Billy Dee Williams will do the role of Malcolm. But then the phone rang. Another sad news was announced, "He's not yet dead, but it's a head wound." The caller referred to Martin. What else has transcribed during that evening, Baldwin hardly remembered. But Bobby Kennedy already announced that Martin was assassinated. He just knew that he sobbed in anger rather than misery. Billy comforted him.

On the day of Martin's wake, people of any sort came. There were Marlon Brando, Sammy Davis, Eartha Kitt, Sidney Poitier, Harry Belafonte, and Coretta King. Baldwin promised himself, since childhood, never to cry in public. It will not do anything, useless. And he was afraid that he cannot stop himself from crying. But pride cannot defeat his emotion. He wept and fell down. It was Sammy who helped him.

Medgar was killed in 1963; Malcolm was assassinated in 1965; and Martin was shot dead in 1968. The three men's names were added to the already growing list of black people who have died for freedom. Baldwin lamented the fact that no record in the law could defend his fellowmen from violence or from murder. He said it in *The Dick Cavett Show in 1968*. He cannot simply relied on the country being a Christian nation since history said it all. It has murdered their ancestors and their brothers. H. Rap Brown, for example, said in 1967 that violence was a necessity in the American culture. He compared it to a cherry pie. Moreover, not only the blacks have demanded freedom in this world. The Irish, the Jewish, the Poles, and the other white races, have also revolutionized and demanded liberty. Even if the struggle was violent, the world appreciated. But when the black population did the exact same thing, they will be tagged as criminals. Dick Cavett also invited a Philosophy professor to argue against Baldwin, Prof. Paul Weiss, from Yale. Paul admitted that he disagreed with many arguments of Baldwin. First, he believed that it was wrong to fight for the right of a certain group of people since man should live his own life, alone. And the problem here was the process of becoming a man. Moreover, he argued that it was misleading to assign people into groups, especially by color, because there were other factors which could be considered in grouping such as interests. But Baldwin defended his belief. Becoming a man was not the main problem. For a Negro, when he attempted to become one, he will face death. This was a dilemma which will not occur in a life of a white man so Paul will not understand. He added that he left America for Paris because he believed that nothing worse could occur on him as compared to what he had experienced in his birthplace. If you wanted to be a man, alone, you can simply isolate yourself from the world you were inhabiting and concentrate on whatever you were doing. But how can a man do that if he was terrified to anything else around him. In America, black people were segregated and hated. The pieces of evidence that he had were the segregation in the Christian church, in the labor unions, in the real estate lobby, and in the school.

America has a confusing definition of democracy. Their definition of it was unimaginable for many people. That was why whatever it was, it was shown in the entertainment industry. But this concept of liberty was not true; it was a fantasy and was better compared to narcotics. It was some sort of escapism. In the U.S. government film, *The Land We Love* (1960), America boasted its scenic beauty, rich history, and infinite opportunities. It was Martin who opposed this fantasy in a rally. He was convincing the government to stop the bombing and to stop the war in Vietnam. To be able to achieve the fantasy they wanted, their mother country has been enslaving other countries and has been stealing its resources. Baldwin supported this argument of Martin regarding the Western countries' hypocrisy. To clear his point, he stated a quote from one of the characters of Dostoyevsky's *The Idiot*. The character said that the wagon which bring bread for humanity might have taken away the food from another part of humanity. The same was true to America. It has no doubt that America was a developed country but at the expense of others, its victims. History will prove it. And these victims, who were often forgotten by the benefactors of the prosperity, were now revolting. It was a perfect reason for a nation's demise since the victims were now battling against the force which oppressed them. They have known their enemy and they were armed with hatred and hope.

The tale of the Negro in America was inseparable to the tale of America. And it was not pleasing to tell. The journey towards the end goal will be bloody and difficult. And the people remained selfish. Their concerns just came out of their mouth. They will not even bother themselves to lift a finger to do some little actions. Their own security and their own money were what matters the most. According to him, the promoted American way of life was a failure.

They can still do something. They just need passion; it was not an abstract thing. It was misleading to think that the horrors this country have experienced were the result of some miscalculations in some numbered formula. For example, criminals were made not because of lack of money; they were created because of the country's lack of passion for them.

This situation of America was undesirable for prophets and angels. It was no longer the land of the free, as according to the popular belief, but the land of the brave. This reality was tolerated by the black people for such a long time that it seemed to be a miracle that they never surrendered. Other people have told the blacks that they were just bitter. But bitterness was not the real deal here because he had all the reasons to be bitter. These included the white people's lack of courage and lack of empathy. And the statement about bitterness just showed an attempt of an unproblematic person to falsify the reality.

Baldwin categorized the experience of the American citizens into two levels. One was represented by Gary Cooper and Doris Day; the other was portrayed by Ray Charles. Gary Cooper was introduced earlier. Doris Day, furthermore, sung a song which reflected the conscious thinking of a white American. She asked herself whether she should be bad or nice to the man who was pleading. The song of the pleading man, or the cry of a Negro, can be echoed by Ray Charles as he was telling a woman to refrain from treating him wrong.

**With all these things, Baldwin warned the country. Its citizen can no longer enslave the black people. They can no longer limit them nor hang them. The processes of captivity and slavery had given the Negro a benefit. It was because the long years of living together allowed the Negro to know their enemies but not the other way around. He knew that not everything could be changed; but to be able to change it, one has to face the problem**

# I Am Not A Nigger

Lastly, Baldwin declared that history was not the things that have occurred in the past. It was the present for the people have shouldered it and the people were the history itself. This fact should not be falsified unless one was a criminal. And he swore that the world was not, was never been, and never will be white. White was just, for him, a description of Chase Manhattan Bank.

In the beginning of this book, Dick Cavett asked why the Negro were not optimistic enough even though there were lots of opportunities for them. Baldwin said that there was no hope if the Americans still use this peculiar language. But back in 1963, he clarified in *The Negro and the American Promise* that he was not a pessimist. If he was a pessimist, he would just accept the belief that the ways of life were already established. But he wanted to change the system for the Negro to survive; so he was required to be an optimist. But it depended greatly on the American people: both from the North and from the South. They have to find out why there was a nigger. Baldwin believed that he was not a nigger nor his fellow black people. They were men. The American people might have invented the term so they should know why. And the future of the blacks relied on them, whether to accept these people whom they have judged for so many years.

# Conclusion

The Negro struggle might had been long gone. People usually know how it started or how it ended. But the stories of the people who have suffered, whether famous or not, were mere blanks in each person's personal memory. This book filled those gaps in history, through James Baldwin's eyes, as it narrated the tales of three black men who have fought for their liberty. It was essential because the lack of knowledge of the past might result to history revisionism.

For Raoul Peck, he wanted to correct his mistakes on understanding of the past and living the present. He was also a victim of history revisionism. He has dedicated his life to search for answers to his questions. He then search for explanations in the words of James Baldwin. And he wanted to retell the explanations he has found in his masterpiece *I Am Not Your Negro*.

For James Baldwin, the awareness of the Negro problem obtained its form at an early age. The country where he was born and where he grew up gave him a wrong impression of the world. It has given him cargoes to carry and future to be afraid of. However, instead of fighting their oppressors, Baldwin flew to Paris. So he felt a sense of guilt when he saw how his fellow Negro continued their daily struggles. He realized that he has to return home and defend their liberty. And so he did.

Although Baldwin's image of a hero was distorted, he seemed to create his very own images of heroes. They were opposite to what the entertainment industry have shown. He did not admit it on his notes but it was apparent. His heroes were black and were not always vengeful. They were Medgar Evers, Malcolm X, and Martin Luther King, Jr. Unfortunately, he lived longer than them because they were murdered. He called himself a witness of their lives and deaths. And since he was one of the last men standing, he thought that it was his duty to create a monument for their legacy. He planned to write a book for them, the *Remember This House*. But he never accomplished it. It was Raoul Peck who succeeded in erecting that monument. Just like what have mentioned earlier, Peck made a film about it, the *I Am Not Your Negro*. And this book allowed the readers to see a glimpse of that movie.

Baldwin narrated the parallel lives and deaths of Medgar, Malcolm, and Martin. They might have opposing actions and opinions but their battle and their fate were all the same. Medgar was a member of the NAACP who investigated criminal cases for his fellow Negro. Malcolm and Martin, on the other hand, were leaders of their groups. The former actually blamed the latter because he promoted love towards their oppressors. But nevertheless, everything that they have done was for the freedom of their fellows. They could have lived longer if this Negro problem never existed.

The process of becoming a man was not the problem. The written laws were not the problem. The racial problem was not the only problem because slavery already ended before Baldwin wrote this book. But its remnants continued. The white people have invented this terrifying problem instead, the Negro problem, to justify their cruelty. They have assigned stereotypes in the body parts of a Negro. Fear was already there in their subconscious minds. And upon seeing a Negro, who was initially a stranger, they have associated their fears to the features of the man. It was ignorance which let them believed that their race should remain pure. Both the black and the white communities hated the things which were interracial. But for an intellectual man such as Baldwin, such interracial events were milestones. They were signs of hope that the black and the white Americans can live peacefully.

However, Baldwin believed that the great future of the black people depended heavily on the white Americans. They should accept the fact that these people they have enslaved and discriminated also built the nation. They were brothers since they have shared the same culture, the same history, the same place. And he left a strong message which echoes until today. They were not niggers; they were humans.

It was also important to dissect the meaning of the title of the film: *I Am Not Your Negro*. Peck might have been thinking that the term "Negro" was an offensive word so it should no longer be used. "Negro" and "nigger" could have been the words which Baldwin called the peculiar language used by the white people. But more importantly, it could also mean that the black people were not under the possession of any white man.

Moreover, at the beginning of the creation of this masterpiece, Gloria Karefa-Smart shared a quote from his brother regarding the new metaphors. Upon reading this book or upon watching the film, a person must realize that white is no longer the metaphor for power, for intellect, or for wealth. Although far from perfect, the world already renewed these metaphors. And these metaphors vary between places and between cultures because the majority of people nowadays respect cultural diversity. The lessons that a reader picked from its pages are also not limited to their impressions towards the black Americans. These can also be applied for other races or other minorities who have experienced discrimination.

# Credits

**I AM NOT YOUR NEGRO**
(93min. USA/France/Belgium/Switzerland)

Directed by Raoul Peck
Written by James Baldwin,
	Compiled and edited by Raoul Peck
Narrated by Samuel L. Jackson

Producers: Rémi Grellety, Raoul Peck, Hébert Peck
Coproducers: Patrick Quinet, Joëlle Bertossa
With the full support and collaboration
	of the James Baldwin Estate

Editor: Alexandra Strauss
Cinematography: Henry Adebonojo, Bill Ross,
	Turner Ross
Animator: Michael Blustein
Sound: Valérie Le Docte, David Gillain
Music: Alexei Aigui
Archival Research: Marie-Hélène Barbéris,
	assisted by Nolwenn Gouault

ARTE France: Fabrice Puchault, Alex Szalat
Executive Producers for ITVS: Sally Jo Fifer, Lois Vossen
Executive Producer for NBPC: Leslie Fields-Cruz

Produced by Velvet Film, INc. (USA), Velvet Film
	(France), Artémis Productions, Close Up Films
In coproduction with ARTE France, Independent Television
Service
	(ITVS) with funding provided by the Corporation for
Public
	Broadcasting (CPB), RTS Radio Télévision Suisse,
RTBF (Télévision
	Belge, Shelter Prod

139

With the support of Centre National du Cinéma et de l'Image Animée,

MEDIA Programme of the European Union, Sundance Institute

Documetary Film Program, National Black Programming

Consortium (NBPC), Cinereach, PROCIREP--Sociéte des

Producteurs, ANGOA, Taxshelter.be, ING, TAX Shelter Incentive of

The Federal Government of Belgium, Cinéforom, Loterie Romande

Sales Agents: ICM Partners, Wide House

# Bibliography

James Baldwin's works used for the narration of *I Am Not Your Negro*;

"As Much Truth As One Can Bear." *New York Times Book Review*, January 14, 1962.
  Collected in *The Cross of Redemption*.
Black English: A Dishonest Argument," In *Black English and the Education of Black*
  *Children and Youth: Proceedings of the National Invitational Symposium on the King Decision*. Detroit: Center for Black Studies, Wayne State University, 1980.  Collected in *The Cross of Redemption*.
*The Cross of Redemption*. New York: Pantheon Books, 2010.
*The Devil Finds Work*. New York: Vintage Books, 1976, 2011.
Letter from James Baldwin to Jay Acton, June 30, 1979. In "Notes Toward Remember
  This House," October 28, 1980.
"Lorraine Hansberry at the Summit." *Freedomways*, no. 19 (1979): 269-72. Collected in
  *The Cross of Redemption*.
"Mass Culture and the Creative Artist: Some Personal Notes." In *Culture for the*
  *Millions: Mass media in Modern Society*, edited by Norman Jacobs. Princeton, N. J.: Van Nostrand, 1959. Collected in *The Cross of Redemption*.
From *Nationalism, Colonialism, and the United States: One Minute to 12!* A Forum
  Sponsored by the Liberation Committee for Africa on Its First Anniversary  Celebration, June 2, 1961. New York: Photo-Offset Press, 1961. Collected in *The Cross of Redemption*.
"The News from All the Northern Cities Is, to Understate It, Grim; the State of the Union
  Is Catastrophic." *New York Times*, April 5, 1978. Collected in *The Cross of Redemption*.

*No Name in the Street.* New York: Vintage Books, 1972.

"Sidney Poitier." *Look,* July 23, 1968. Collected in *The Cross of Redemption.*

"The White problem." In 100 *Years of Emancipation,* edited by Robert A. Goodwin.

Chicago: Rand McNally, 1964. Collected in *The Cross of Redemption.*

# Permissions

# Illustrations

1 Malcolm X(Burt Shavitz/The LIFE Images Collection/Getty Images)

2 Martin Luther King, Jr., with family (pam koner-yohai/Corbis Premium
Historical/Getty Images)

3 Medgar Evers (Private Collection/Bridgeman Images)

4 Three young men protesting desegration (AP Images)

5 Dorothy Counts (The Charlotte Observer)

6 Joan Crawford in *Dance, Fools, Dance*, 1931 (MGM)

7 Clinton Rosemond in *They Won't Forget*, 1937 (Warner Bros.)

8 John Wayne in *Stagecoach*, 1939 (United Artists)

9 James Baldwin at his typewriter in Istanbul, 1964 (© sedatpakay.com)

10 Demonstrators and police in Selma (© Spider Martin)

11 Martin Luther King, Jr., and Malcolm X shaking hands (Bettmann/Bettman?Getty
Images)

12 Lorraine Hansberry (Afro Newspaper/Gado/Archive Photos/Getty Images)

13 *Jackson Daily News,* June 12, 1963

14 Fredi Washington in *Imitation of Life*, 1934 (Universal Pictures)

15 Cumberland Landing, Virgina. Group at Mr. Foller's farm, by James F. Gibson, 1862.
(Library of Congress)

16 Richard Widmark in *No way Out*, 1950 (20th Century Fox)

17 Sidney Poitier and Tony Curtis in *The Defiant Ones*, 1958 (United Artists)

18 Still from Chiquita banana advertisement (© Streamline Films, Inc.)

19 Sidney Poitier in *Guess Who's Coming to Dinner*, 1967 (Columbia Pictures)

20 Sidney Poitier smiling (at Rod Steiger) in *In the heat of the Night,* 1967 (United

Artists)

21 Rod Steiger smiling (at Sidney Poitier) in *In the Heat of the Night*, 1967 (United
Artists)

22 From *The Secret of Selling the Negro* (Courtesy of Johnson Publishing Company,
LLC. All rights reserved.)

23 From *The Secret of Selling the Negro* (Courtesy of Johnson Publishing Company,
LLC. All, rights reserved.)

24 James Baldwin at Cambridge University debate with William F. Buckley, 1965 (The
Cambridge Union Society/BBC/Getty Images)

25 John Wayne in *The Searchers,* 1956 (John Springer Collection/Corbis Historical/getty
Images)

26 family in front of house, Kodak, 1958

27 Black Panther raid, August 30, 1970, D. Ligato, photographer *(Philadelphia Evening
Bulletin*/Special Collections Research Center, Template University Libraries,
Philadelphia, PA)

28 Coretta Scott King and her family at coffin of Martin Luther King, Jr. (© Costa
Manos/Magnum Photos)

29 Woman crying at memorial for Martin Luther King, Jr. (© Bob Adelman)

30 mug shot of Ben McDaniel (National Archives)

31 Mug shot of Preston James (National Archives)

32 Rodney King beating March 3, 1991

33 Doris Day in *Lullaby of Broadway,* 1951 (Warner Bros.)

34 Ray Charles, "What'd I Say"

35 Doris Day in *Lover Come Back,* 1961 (Universal Pictures)

36 The lynching of Laura Nelson, May 25, 1911, Okemah, Oklahoma (Oklahoma
Historical Society)

37 James Baldwin in *The Negro and the American Promise,* 2004

(WGBH)

# Final Thoughts

Hey! Did you enjoy this book? We sincerely hope you thoroughly enjoyed this short read and have gotten immensely valuable insights that will help you in any areas of your life.

Would it be too greedy if we ask for a review from you?

It takes 1 minute to leave 1 review to possibly influence 1 more person's decision to read just 1 book which may change their 1 life. Your 1 minute matters and we value it and thank you so much for giving us your 1 minute. If it sucks, just say it sucks. Period.

# FREE BONUS

## P.S. Is it okay if we overdeliver?

Here at Abbey Beathan Publishing, we believe in overdelivering way beyond our reader's expectations. Is it okay if we overdeliver?

Here's the deal, we're going to give you an extremely valuable cheatsheet of "Accelerated Learning". We've partnered up with Ikigai Publishing to present to you the exclusive bonus of "Accelerated Learning Cheatsheet"

What's the catch? We need to trust you… You see, we want to overdeliver and in order for us to do that, we've to trust our reader to keep this bonus a secret to themselves. Why? Because we don't want people to be getting our exclusive accelerated learning cheatsheet without even buying our books itself. Unethical, right?

Ok. Are you ready?

Simply Visit this link: http://bit.ly/acceleratedcheatsheet

We hope you'll enjoy our free bonuses as much as we've enjoyed preparing it for you!

# Free Bonus #2: Free Book Preview of Summary: Why Buddhism is True
## The Book at a Glance

"Why Buddhism Is True: The Science and Philosophy of Meditation" is about the connections of Buddhist teachings to scientific facts about the human mind. Its main focus is on mindfulness meditation and how it can help people overcome problems and eventually attain liberation from suffering. To accomplish its goal of showing people the path towards freedom, the book gives numerous scientific studies on human psychology, testimonials from meditators such as Robert Wright himself, and helpful tips to practice Buddhist teachings in daily life. The book starts with an epigraph: an excerpt of "A Dream Play" by August Strindberg and is divided into 16 chapters about the following.

1 Taking the Red Pill

Wright describes the Buddhist tradition as similar to the red pill in the movie "The Matrix".

2 Paradoxes of Meditation

There are paradoxes in meditation and Buddhism that make sense experientially.

3 When Are Feelings Illusions?

Feelings contribute to our delusions; this chapter explains how and why.

4 Bliss, Ecstasy, and More Important Reasons to Meditate

Meditation can provide intense feelings of bliss, but there are other important benefits to it.

5 The Alleged Nonexistence of Your Self

The Buddha spoke of the self as illusory; this chapter examines this statement.

6 Your CEO Is MIA

The CEO in the chapter title stands for the controller of the body and the mind, and it appears to be non-existent.

7 The Mental Modules That Run Your Life

According to experiments and observations, the mind is not a unit but is composed of numerous modules, and they control what we think, feel, and do.

8 How Thoughts Think Themselves

This chapter explains what activates thoughts and why they behave the way they do.

9 "Self" Control

In here, self-control is examined and considered in the light of mental modules.

10 Encounters with the Formless

The formless is a Buddhist concept that causes profound insights.

11 The Upside of Emptiness

Being empty is the natural state of things; although this may seem negative, it is actually beneficial.

12 A Weedless World

Wright hates a particular kind of weed, but his meditative practices caused him to appreciate his old plant enemy.

13 Like, Wow, Everything Is One (at Most)

Hindus believe in the Oneness of everything; Buddhists believe in everything – this chapter explains why they may both be right.

14 Nirvana in a Nutshell

This chapter talks about Nirvana or enlightenment – the ultimate aspiration of Buddhists and everyone who seeks liberation.

15 Is Enlightenment Enlightening?

Chapter fifteen takes a closer look at enlightenment.

16 Meditation and the Unseen Order

The unseen order is theorized to be something that we must align ourselves into; the final chapter explains how mediation can achieve that.

# Epigraph

Writer: But tell me before you go. What was the worst thing about being down here?

Agnes: Just existing. Knowing my sight was blurred by my eyes, my hearing dulled by my ears, and my bright thought trapped in the grey maze of a brain. Have you seen a brain?

Writer: And you're telling me that's what's wrong with us? How else can we be?

- A Dream Play by August Strindberg, as adapted by Caryl Churchill

# A Note to Readers

Since a book with a title such as "Why Buddhism Is True" needs careful qualifications, Robert Wright sets five things clear:

1.  Wright didn't discuss about the supernatural aspects of Buddhism (such as reincarnation) but only its naturalistic parts – the ideas that fit within philosophy and modern psychology. Despite this, he wants you to take Buddhism's extraordinary claims seriously because they can revolutionize how you view yourself and the world.

2.  Wright focused on common fundamental ideas found across different Buddhist traditions, which vary in emphasis, doctrines, and forms.

3.  Wright didn't delve into the finer parts of Buddhist philosophy and psychology.

4.  Although Wright recognizes the trickiness of using the word "true" since claims of truth should be met with scepticism (this is an important lesson in Buddhism), he believes that the word still has a place in Buddhist thought. He argues that even Buddha gave Four Noble Truths, and that Buddhism's evaluation of and remedy to the human predicament are correct, valid, and important.

5. Wright claims that asserting core Buddhist concepts' validity doesn't automatically say anything about other philosophical or spiritual traditions. He adds that there may be logical tensions between an idea in Buddhism and one from another tradition, but oftentimes there aren't any. He quotes the Dalai Lama in saying that one shouldn't try to apply what he/she learns from Buddhism to become a better Buddhist, but to become a better whatever-the-person-already-is.